AGAINST IMPERIALISM

GREG JOHNSON

Counter-Currents Publishing Ltd.
San Francisco
2023

Copyright © 2023 by Counter-Currents Publishing
All rights reserved

Cover image by Wave Guy, https://t.me/waveguy

Cover design by Kevin I. Slaughter

Published in the United States by
COUNTER-CURRENTS PUBLISHING LTD.
http://www.counter-currents.com/

Hardcover ISBN: 978-1-64264-028-1
Paperback ISBN: 978-1-64264-029-8
E-book ISBN: 978-1-64264-030-4

Contents

Preface ❖ iii

Against Imperialism

1. Against Imperialism ❖ 1
2. Against White Unionism ❖ 12
3. One White State or Many? ❖ 22
4. Reply to Gregory Hood ❖ 30

The Ukraine War

5. Russia & Ukraine, Again ❖ 43
6. What's Really at Stake in Ukraine ❖ 51
7. The Ukraine War, One Last Time ❖ 60
8. Questions on NATO, Russia, & Ukraine ❖ 66
9. The Dugin Assassination ❖ 76
10. Nationalism for All ❖ 81

Two Notes on Sovereignty

11. Might, Right, & Sovereignty ❖ 86
12. Notes on Sovereignty & International Order ❖ 90

White Identity Politics

13. Tucker Carlson on White Identity Politics ❖ 101
14. Christopher Rufo on White Identity Politics ❖ 107
15. In Your Heart, You Know Ye's Right ❖ 119
16. How I Got Banned from the New "Free Speech" Twitter ❖ 125
17. Dave Chappelle, Non-White Ally of 2022 ❖ 128
18. Why White Nationalists Didn't Want a Red Wave ❖ 141
19. Trump 2024: A Bad Idea Whose Time has Come ❖ 145
20. Palestinians & Jews, Again ❖ 149
21. Abortion & White Nationalism, Again ❖ 154
22. Is it Rational for Blacks to Distrust Whites? ❖ 159

23. When Richard Hanania Wrote for
Counter-Currents ❖ 163

OUR MOVEMENT

24. Politics vs. Self-Help ❖ 168
25. Racial Solidarity & Moral Hazard ❖ 175
26. Revolution with Full Benefits ❖ 180
27. Thinking of Quitting the Movement? ❖ 184
28. How to Leave the Movement ❖ 190
29. Turning the World Around ❖ 196
30. Reasons for Optimism ❖ 198

Index ❖ 201

About the Author ❖ 210

Preface

Against Imperialism collects thirty pieces of political commentary written primarily in 2022 and 2023 and published at *Counter-Currents*.

Many of these pieces are parts of online debates, but six were occasioned by actual live debates. "One White State or Many" and "Reply to Gregory Hood" are from a debate with Gregory Hood on "Ethnonationalism vs. Imperialism" on June 10, 2023, moderated by Cyan Quinn. "Russia & Ukraine, Again" and "What's Really at Stake in Ukraine" are from a debate with E. Michael Jones on the Ukraine War on March 26, 2022, organized and moderated by Fróði Midjord. "The Ukraine War, One Last Time" and "Questions on NATO, Russia, & Ukraine" are from a debate with Mark Collett on October 15, 2022, organized and hosted by Joel Davis. I wish to thank my opponents as well as the organizers and moderators.

I also wish to thank John Morgan, Collin Cleary, James O'Meara, and David Zsutty for helping edit and proof this collection; Jef Costello and Fróði Midjord for their promotional quotes; Wave Guy[1] for the cover art and Kevin Slaughter for creating the cover; and the many writers, donors, and commenters at *Counter-Currents* who make all my work possible.

This book is dedicated to the memory of Serhiy Zaikovsky: guide, translator, and hero of Ukraine.

Christmas Eve 2023

---

[1] https://t.me/waveguy

Against Imperialism

One of the fundamental divisions in the White Nationalist movement is between ethnonationalists and imperialists. Ethnonationalists want a world in which every distinct people has the right to a sovereign homeland. Imperialists want a single white racial state. Wilmot Robertson makes the case for ethnonationalism in his book *The Ethnostate*, whereas Francis Parker Yockey presents the case for imperialism in *Imperium*. Other advocates of imperialism include Sir Oswald Mosley, Jean Thiriart, and Guillaume Faye.

The division between imperialists and ethnonationalists is often overlooked. Both ethnonationalists and imperialists largely agree on what we dislike, and every day our enemies deliver fresh outrages to occupy our attention. By contrast, creating white ethnostates, or a unified white imperium, will only happen in the future. Why quarrel about long-term differences when we can focus on shared concerns in the present?

There's also a muddle-headedness about the imperialist position that makes it easy to ignore. I have lost count of the times I have heard the imperialist argument put forward and then taken back at the last moment by saying we need "an imperium . . . or maybe a federation . . . or maybe an alliance" as if there is no essential difference between a single white state and a group of white states in a federation or an alliance.

There are plenty of differences between white advocates that are best set aside for the common good of the race, such as Christians versus pagans, pro-abortion versus anti-abortion, or capitalists versus socialists. There have been healthy white societies on both sides of such questions, so White Nationalists are not forced to choose between them. Different white homelands could take different positions on these issues.

But we must deal with the question of imperialism versus ethnonationalism. The two options are mutually exclusive. If there is only one white state, there can't be many. So we must choose.

Why can't we be simply "pro-white"? Because if we are serious about pro-white politics, we must give that a *concrete* meaning, and that means answering the question of one state or many.

Moreover, since this is a question about our ultimate goals, it is about the essence of our movement. What makes us a movement rather than a gaggle of fellow travelers is having a common political goal. Fellow travelers have different ultimate goals but find themselves temporarily on the same path. They might share common complaints and enemies. They may be allies and companions for the time being. But because they have different destinations, they will eventually arrive at a fork in the road, where they will have to shake hands and part ways.

The freshest statement of the imperialist position is Gregory Hood's recent American Renaissance speech "The Challenge Ahead": "What I want is a united Western Civilization-State that will ensure the physical survival of our race."[1]

A "civilization-state" is a new geopolitical term for an empire that defines itself in opposition to Western liberal democracy. Putin's Russia and Xi's China are the preeminent examples. Both are empires encompassing many nations under the cultural and political hegemony of a founding people: the Russians and Han Chinese. A white civilization state would presumably follow the same pattern: an empire embracing many peoples under the politi-

---

[1] Gregory Hood, "The Challenge Ahead," Parts I and II, *American Renaissance*, December 15 and 20, 2022.

cal and cultural domination of a founding people.

I usually agree with Greg Hood, but not in this case. I don't want a single white state for the reasons Wilmot Robertson sets forth in *The Ethnostate*: ethnonationalism promotes peace and diversity (political, cultural, and genetic), whereas imperialism imperils peace and diversity. A single white state will not emerge without conflict. Such a struggle is the last thing that a race demographically collapsing toward extinction needs.

This prospect is especially horrifying given the prime candidates for *Herrenvolk*: Germans, Russians, and Americans. These nations might have the power to establish and dominate a white imperium, but culturally and spiritually, they are among the most degenerate. Increasing their power would make almost every European nation worse off rather than better.

Hood claims that the imperium he envisions would respect "local cultures," but this is hardly reassuring, given the record of empires past and present. Nor is it reassuring when Hood remarks that, "We have been one people before the relatively new phenomena of national identity and Christian denominational differences divided us."

When imperialists say national identities are "relatively new," it is like Leftists saying they are "social constructs": they are slated for destruction. Moreover, the lost unity that Hood mourns didn't always exist. Yes, much of Europe was basically one people—after Rome homogenized it. Yes, much of Europe was also Roman Catholic—after the church destroyed all its rivals. So much for "respecting local cultures."

There are four principal arguments for imperialism. First, only a unified white state can secure a future for the white race. Second, nation states and national identities are obsolete in an increasingly globalized world. Third, we are attacked as whites, so we must defend ourselves as whites; more specific ethnic and national identities don't matter. Fourth, empires are glorious! Just think of Rome, Napoleon, Warhammer 40K.

Let's look at how Hood reprises the classic imperialist tropes. He touches on the first three arguments in a single paragraph:

> National identities themselves are relatively recent creations. They are fading with travel, technology, and geopolitical arrangements that are breaking down the nation-state. The multipolar world that is emerging is a battle between civilizations. What unites a white person in America, England, France, Germany, Italy, the Netherlands, South Africa, Australia, and every other place is stronger than what unites him to those of different races who carry the same passport. As the world becomes more connected technologically, race isn't fading. It's becoming more important, and it's our opponents who insist it is central to every social interaction. We didn't ask for this. We're only playing the cards we were dealt.

The first argument for imperialism is that small states are weaker than large states. Therefore, to protect themselves from large non-white powers like China, small white states must amalgamate into a single white empire. As Hood puts it, "This is not a dream. It's a necessity. Whites are a hated, shrinking, global minority. We need a geopolitical lifeboat capable of ensuring our physical existence." Our choice is literally "join or die."

Whites should definitely be concerned with geopolitical competition from other races and civilizations. But at best this is an argument for shifting military alliances or more permanent treaty organization like NATO. It falls far short of an argument for a single white state. There is simply no power on earth that requires the political unification of all white nations to resist it.

Beyond that, wars and other geopolitical crises are by their very nature interruptions in the normal order of things. They are temporary and fluid. It is foolish to institute permanent and fixed solutions to preempt temporary and fluid problems. Why would any nation permanently surrender its sovereignty to a superstate because of the *possibility* that it might lose its sovereignty in a war with China?

After all, surrendering sovereignty entails dangers too. If a nation-state surrenders its sovereignty to a superstate, that virtually guarantees that alien peoples will have far more power to determine its destiny—again, to avoid the mere possibility of domination by still more alien peoples. This increases the chance that one's culture will be homogenized and one's population and resources will be stripped by the imperial capital. One will also risk being dragged into unnecessary wars.

Another problem with a superstate is that it puts all our eggs in one basket. If the future of the white race depends on the decisions of a single government, what happens if that government goes catastrophically wrong? Obviously, that would imperil the whole race. In such a situation, Hood's "geopolitical lifeboat" would be more like a geopolitical *Titanic*, right down to the hubris, and individual nation-states would be the true lifeboats.

Imperialists, however, argue that nation-states are fading away due to globalization. They will certainly disappear if nothing is done to stop globalization. But this is an argument for resisting globalization, not going along with it.

Francis Parker Yockey poured scorn on tiny "comic opera" states. He equated national sovereignty simply with power, which means only very large states have sovereignty. Of course, since even the largest state can be destroyed if the rest of the world allies against it, that means that no nations have sovereignty, which is a *reductio ad absurdum* of equating sovereignty and power. Yockey simply can't explain why some of the statelets he mocks, like Lichtenstein and Monaco, are among the oldest and most prosperous sovereign entities on the planet, even though they are also among the weakest. But life isn't constant war.

Sovereignty is not power. It is a moral norm. In international law, a sovereign state is the equivalent of a moral person, namely someone who bears rights. Sovereign states are masters of their own internal affairs. No matter their size, they are considered to be equal under international law.

To say that small nations have no sovereignty is as incoherent as saying that weak people have no rights. Rights don't make you bullet proof. But they do provide guidelines of proper behavior. Strong nations might invade weak nations, but the idea of sovereignty means they are *wrong* to do so, and other nations are *right* to join together to resist them. Sovereign nations are not in a state of perpetual war, because moral norms matter, even to politicians.

The idea of sovereignty is as old as political thought, but the modern concept of sovereignty was created in the seventeenth century to bring an end to the religious wars by, in effect, disempowering the pope to meddle in the internal religious affairs of nations. The purpose was to promote peace by guaranteeing *the right to differ*.

Despite globalist clichés about the inevitable decline of the nation-state, it is still the foundation of global political order. Nation states make war and peace. They educate their citizens. They regulate the media. They open and close borders. They regulate economic activity. They can bring oligarchs to heel. They control virtually all the institutions and incentives necessary to preserve or destroy their populations.

The various "globalist" treaty organizations, customs unions, and alliances are based upon agreements among sovereign nation-states. They would evaporate overnight if enough nation-states walked away from them.

If white advocates are serious about saving our race, we need to challenge the current establishment at all levels, the higher the better, with the holy grail being control of sovereign states, which can say "no" to subsidiary powers, fellow sovereign states, and globalist entities. With enough sovereign states on our side, we can turn the world around.

Imperialists also argue that nation-states are increasingly irrelevant because national identities are fading away. But this is simply another argument for resisting globalization rather than giving in to it. Beyond that, cultural homogenization is largely superficial. Yes, Europeans increasingly consume the same goods, but there will always be different European peoples, because national identity is passed along with one's mother tongue. English may be today's *lingua franca*, but that's nothing new. In the past it was French or Latin. But English will not be adopted by everyone, and it will remain a second or third language to most of those who learn it.

Hood argues that racial identity will eclipse national identity simply because whites are being attacked *as a race* and replaced *as a race*. "Our fate will be decided as whites. Thus, we must act as whites. It will not be as members of different nations." But this does not follow.

Yes, we are being attacked as a race. Therefore, we need to fight back on the racial front. When you are attacked, your enemy gets to choose where and how he attacks you, and you must respond in kind.

But just because our enemies see us as nothing but whites, that doesn't mean they are right. There's more to our identity than just race. Language, culture, and ethnicity also matter.

Hood, however, seems to allow our enemies to define us: "Being white is the most meaningful identity we have. Our rulers gave us a negative one. We need a positive one." Because of this, Hood argues that "we are a people, not simply a group of peoples," and one people needs one state.

But whites are a race, not a people, because peoplehood presupposes a common language and culture, whereas whites have many different languages and cultures, alongside a common genetic and cultural heritage. White Nationalism, therefore, cannot mean one white state for one white people. Instead, it can only mean national self-determination for all white peoples.

Hood likens his dream to the Roman Empire, which he thinks was glorious. I confess it leaves me cold. The Roman Empire left magnificent ruins, but it was a catastrophe for the peoples it conquered. Julius Caesar alone killed more than a million Gauls—at a time when one had to look one's victims in the eye—to add France to the Roman Empire. No white empire has even been created without spilling oceans of white blood, on all sides. For a dying race, this is sheer madness. Thus it is a fair question: How many millions of Europeans are today's imperialists willing to kill to create their dream?

Hood makes it very clear that we can't just defer debating imperialism vs. ethnonationalism forever. One's answer will define the essence of our movement and determine the meaning of everything we do today:

> There are more white advocates than ever, all looking for something to do, all pushing in a million different directions. We must have a final goal that gives us a common direction, even if we disagree on tactics, ideology, or organizational missions. The Western Imperium, the sacral empire that would unite and protect the white race, is that final goal.

Of course, one danger of insisting that all white advocates pursue the same goal is that fewer people will get involved. But this is a debate that we cannot avoid. Moreover, if one chooses imperialism, we will not be able to defer all the other divisive questions either. For if there is only one white state, there can be only one answer to such questions as capitalism vs. socialism.

Another reason we can't defer the imperialism vs. ethnonationalism question is that one's attitudes on this matter influence one's present-day political stances. Although imperialists often present themselves as utopian dreamers, they are often apologists for quite grubby contemporary power agglomerations, as long as they are opposed to ethnonationalism.

For instance, before abandoning the Right altogether, Richard Spencer was a well-known standard bearer for imperialism. From 2013 on, Spencer favored Russian imperialism over Ukrainian nationalism, the United Kingdom over an independent Scotland, the European Union over an independent United Kingdom, and Spain over an independent Catalonia. It was certainly consistent, but what did it have to do with white advocacy?

Currently the white race is facing extinction though low fertility, miscegenation, and replacement migration imposed by the existing political establishment, which exercises power through both national and transnational institutions. To save ourselves, we need to replace the establishment before it replaces us. That means that we need power. Which means we need to contest power at all levels.

But Spencer's imperialism led him to denigrate even explicitly pro-white ethnonationalist movements as "petty" while defending anti-white imperial agglomerations simply because they are larger and more powerful. This makes no sense if one's primary concern is white survival. Indeed, it only makes sense if one is primarily a power worshipper, which is what Spencer turned out to be. This is why he left the dissident Right altogether. He followed the power.

Hood's imperialism also leads to incoherence in the face of present-day politics:

> What is to be done? We will build tribes, churches, networks. We will turn our backs on their world and build our own. . . . We will build political power locally and wield it where we can. And we will build towards the dream of a Western Imperium that is our destiny, that will bind our people together in unity, honor, and strength.

Hood counsels us here to think both very big and very small. "Building strength locally is a first step, and it allows for political action." This is true. But if one can organize locally, why not regionally and nationally as well? How can one get from the local to the universal without passing through the nation-state?

Hood clearly thinks that demographic change is too advanced in the United States for a pro-white force to gain national power. (The proper lesson for Americans is to give up on democracy, not America.)

But in most white countries, it is still possible for pro-white forces to vie for national power. Why pass up the chance? Why seek power only on the local level, which can be annulled on the national level, but not seek national power within existing sovereign states?

Because this is the logic of the imperialist dream: "Our fate will be decided as whites. Thus, we must act as whites. It will not be as members of different nations." To believe in the imperium commits one to the idea that there's no point in contesting power in nation-states, even though that is where actual sovereignty resides. This is simply self-defeating.

In sum, I advocate ethnonationalism because I believe that it promotes peace and diversity by giving distinct peoples their own sovereign homelands. I oppose imperialism because it increases conflict and decreases diversity. Moreover, I have explained why I don't find the arguments for preferring imperialism to ethnonationalism convincing. Finally, ethnonationalism is politically realistic because it can build upon existing political movements and existing sovereign states, whereas imperialism offers high-minded rhetoric but no concrete path to white survival.

The debate between imperialists and ethnonationalists cannot be avoided, because it concerns the very essence of our movement. Indeed, are we one movement or two? Nor can the debate be postponed, because one's answer has concrete implications for the movement today. I look forward to continuing the conversation.

Counter-Currents, December 27, 2022

AGAINST WHITE UNIONISM

I wish to respond to Asier Abadroa's critique of my essay "Against Imperialism," which he has entitled "White Nationalism vs. Racially Conscious White Ethnonationalisms."[1]

IMPERIALISM

Abadroa thinks it is a bad idea for advocates of a single white state, like Francis Parker Yockey or Gregory Hood, to call themselves "imperialists":

> First, we must categorically reject the term "imperialist" as a designation for someone who wants a single white nation. Francis Parker Yockey is far from representing the majority of this tendency's supporters, and the word "imperialism" has a negative psychological charge due to its association with such concepts as one ethnic group imposing itself by force on others, or an absolute hegemony by one ethnic group over others.

Abadroa, instead, wishes to use the terms "White Nationalism" or "White Unionism." I will use "White Unionism" here, since I call my own position White Nationalism. He stipulates that White Unionism won't have the bad traits associated with imperialism, namely coercion, cultural homogenization, and the domination of one ethnic group over others.

---

[1] Asier Abadroa, "White Nationalism vs. Racially Conscious White Ethnonationalisms," Parts 1 and 2, *Counter-Currents*, January 9 and 10.

WHITE NATIONALISM

Abadroa objects to my definition of White Nationalism as the right of all white peoples to their own sovereign homelands:

> Let's not forget that the term *nationalist* in our milieu is always accompanied by the adjective referring to that which the individual considers his or her nation. I consider the white race to be my nation, and therefore, I am a White Nationalist. But, if someone considers his nation to be that of a particular ethnicity, in what sense can he call himself a White Nationalist? To say, "I am a White Nationalist and I want independence for my ethnicity" is as contradictory as saying "I am a Spanish nationalist and I want independence for my Basque Country," or for a Scot to say "I am a British nationalist and I want independence for my Scotland." It just doesn't make sense.

I don't think my concept of White Nationalism is problematic, for two reasons.

First, a race is not a nation, it is a biological group. To be a nation, a group needs several traits.

1. They must be biologically related.
2. They must share a common consciousness, meaning primarily a common culture and a common mother tongue. (Mother tongue = first language.)

Whites are biologically related, but we do not share a common mother language. We have a common cultural heritage, but we also have many distinct cultures. Therefore, whites are not a nation. Whites are many nations. We call a group that is both biologically related and united by a common consciousness an ethnic group.

As an ethnonationalist, I believe that different ethnic groups are the proper bearers of sovereignty, as opposed to the many peoples encompassed in multicultural states. A sovereign people can live how they like in their own homeland. They don't have to ask anyone's permission to be themselves, and if outside forces interfere with a sovereign nation, such forces have done something wrong.

The sovereignty of peoples is a moral concept analogous to the rights of individuals: both concepts provide boundaries. These boundaries proscribe force, promote cooperation, and create zones of freedom where both nations and individuals can live as they see fit, consistent with the rights of others to do the same. (To understand how my idea of sovereignty differs from that of Abadroa, see my articles "Might, Right, and Sovereignty" and "Notes on Sovereignty and International Order," which are chapters 5 and 6 below.)

A group's culture can be likened to an individual's personality. Individuals seek to have their own lives and their own spaces because sharing a household, a bedroom, or a kitchen with others can lead to needless tensions and conflicts that simply disappear when we have our own spaces. The same is true for different ethnic groups living in the same country, under the same rules. As William Blake put it, "One law for the lion and ox is oppression." The solution is separation. This is why peoples who live in multiethnic nations seek independence.[2]

Abadroa is simply wrong to claim that the world is trending away from nationalism. The number of sovereign states has increased dramatically over the last century. Beyond that, there's nothing inevitable about glob-

---

[2] For more in this vein, see Alan Smithee, "Ethnonationalism for Normies," *Counter-Currents*, July 1, 2016.

alization erasing national borders and identities. That might make it easier for shoppers and refugees, but states simply need to summon the political will to say "no." We can share recipes and trade goods without erasing borders and peoples.

If you want the white race to become a single ethnic group, this is akin to declaring existing white ethnicities to be merely the raw materials from which a new people can be fashioned. Why would any self-respecting people consent to that? Making whites into a single ethnic group requires cultural and linguistic homogenization, which looks a lot like ethnic domination by the people whose mother tongue is being imposed. Moreover, such a program will create an inevitable backlash, at which point its advocates will either have to abandon it or resort to coercion. You may not wish to call this imperialism, but the substance is the same.

Second, there is no contradiction in saying "I am a White Nationalist, and I want a sovereign homeland for my particular people." Why talk about race at all if you are simply a Spanish or an Austrian nationalist? Because of "naturalization." Every state makes provisions for outsiders to become citizens. We are now being told that non-whites can become Spaniards and Austrians through naturalization. So we have to remind them that only whites can be naturalized as members of European nations (and only in small numbers, and only if they "assimilate" the local culture, a process that generally requires several generations). Just as there are Spanish civic nationalists and multiculturalists, there should also be Spanish White Nationalists to remind them that whiteness is a necessary condition for being part of any European nation.[3]

---

[3] See my essay "Why 'White' Nationalism?" in *Toward a New Nationalism*, 2nd ed. (San Francisco: Counter-Currents, 2023).

THE UNITED STATES

Abadroa expresses some confusions about the nature of America and American nationalism. In such articles as "American Ethnic Identity"[4] and "What Is American Nationalism?"[5] I argue that Americans are a distinct European people, blended from different European stocks. We are not English. We have our own language (American English) and our own culture (for better or worse). Americans, I hasten to add, are a white nation. Blacks, Asians, Amerindians, and Mestizos living within America's borders are not Americans. They are either distinct peoples (for instance, Indian tribes and black Americans) or members of other nations who have simply crossed our borders (for instance, Mestizos and various Asian groups).

As an ethnonationalist, I support a combination of partition and repatriation to solve America's diversity problem. There should be at least one white American nation. There may be multiple ones, depending on how the current system crumbles. I would not object to the South rising again, but I wonder if there are enough actual Southerners left in Dixie for something like that to happen. There should be a nation for black Americans. The various Amerindian nations should be able to keep their reservations. I also support repatriation of post-1965 immigrant populations. Opening our borders to the world was a mistake that simply needs to be rectified.[6] But it will be a "no fault" divorce.[7] We won't demand reparations.

---

[4] Greg Johnson, "American Ethnic Identity," in *In Defense of Prejudice*, Foreword by Tito Perdue (San Francisco: Counter-Currents, 2017).

[5] In *Toward a New Nationalism*.

[6] See Greg Johnson, "Restoring White Homelands," in *The White Nationalist Manifesto* (San Francisco: Counter-Currents, 2018).

[7] See Greg Johnson, "Irreconcilable Differences: The Case for

FEDERALISM

Abadroa claims that ethnonationalist fears of cultural homogenization in a single white state can be handled with "federalism":

> . . . there is no reason why a federal nation could not grant autonomy in such matters to various territories within it. If China under the Communist dictatorship had special economic zones where capitalism was practiced freely as an experiment—and whose economic model has since been copied to a large extent by the rest of the country—then surely this autonomy can also be granted within a white nation, even at the most local level, such as cities or counties.
>
> In fact, pilot projects are sometimes carried out in only a few towns or cities, and this is something that I believe should be developed to its full potential, especially as an excellent vehicle for reducing people's sense of alienation. If it were to be decided, there is no reason why within each ethnic federated state there cannot be anarchist micro-societies, homosexual villages, Amish reservations, pagan communities, or anything else where there is sufficient demand. Therefore, a federal nation can be politically, culturally, and genetically as diverse as several independent ethnostates.

My issue is with this language of "granting autonomy." Abadroa envisions a single white state "granting" local autonomy to distinct peoples to speak their own languages, celebrate their own holidays and heroes, and educate their children to do the same. Of course, existing

---

Racial Divorce," in *Truth, Justice, & a Nice White Country* (San Francisco: Counter-Currents, 2015).

nations do this as a matter of sovereign right. They don't have to ask anyone's permission. Why would they surrender their sovereignty to a centralized state from which they would then petition to be granted permission to do what they used to do as a matter of right? Why would a sovereign Italian nation accept the status of a mere Italian reservation, a status that can be granted or revoked by a central state?

Federalism is a very slippery concept. It is a hybrid of *a confederation* and a *unified sovereign state with devolved powers*. A confederation is a group of sovereign states that have delegated certain powers to a central government, for instance to organize common policies for defense, foreign affairs, money, weights and measures, etc. In a confederation, sovereignty remains with the states that enter into the agreement. A unified sovereign state can devolve (or concentrate) its powers at will, and such decisions do not hinge on "sufficient demand," since that would imply that sovereignty is in the hands of any group that wants it, rather than in the hands of the central state.

Federalism is an attempt to split the difference. Federalists think they can give some sovereignty to the central government and some to lesser jurisdictions. But sovereignty cannot be divided. Sovereign states can delegate their powers to a central government. Or a central sovereign state can devolve powers to local communities. But sovereignty can't rest in both places. What if the states disagree with the central government on a matter of great importance? Sovereignty lies with the party that takes precedence. Sovereignty lies with the party that can say "no." If the central government can say "no," then sovereignty resides there. If the constituent states can say "no," then sovereignty resides there. What if a federal system does not anticipate such a conflict and makes no provisions for its resolution, perhaps out of a desire not to take a stand on where sovereignty ultimately lies? Eventually, such conflicts will be settled by force.

This is precisely the path America followed to its Civil War. In the South, the states believed they retained sovereignty and had the power to nullify federal laws they regarded as unconstitutional. In the North, the federal government, specifically the federal judiciary, claimed to be the highest authority on the interpretation of law. This conflict could not be solved within the existing constitutional framework, so the South seceded, and the North went to war to stop them.

Why would anyone create such an unstable "federal" hybrid? Short-sightedness and anti-intellectualism can't be ruled out. Most politicians are more concerned with pleasing people than with intellectual consistency. Americans especially have a tendency to avoid tough decisions and force future generations to pay the price. For what it is worth, though, the anti-federalists feared that the new Constitution was merely the first step by which predominantly Northern and mercantile elites would create a consolidated, imperial state. It turns out they were right. The process of consolidation was completed by Abraham Lincoln, to the ruin of Constitution and Confederacy alike. The lesson is that sometimes, sovereign states enter empires voluntarily, often deceived as much by their own hopes as the imperialists' guile. Force comes into play only when they want to leave.

The European Union

The European Union, like the United States before the Civil War, is an inherently unstable "federal" hybrid. It began as a confederation of sovereign states. But the eventual goal of the EU was clear from the start: to gradually strip the constituent states of their sovereignty and establish itself as a consolidated sovereign superstate. The EU is not a sovereign state yet, however, which is why the United Kingdom could leave and, arguably, why other states still wish to join. But as the EU's drive toward consolidating sovereign power continues, it may set the stage for the next great European civil war. This is why I disagree with Abadroa's views on the EU:

> Despite not being governed by the people and political ideas we want, the closest example there is of a united white nation at present is the European Union. Not only has it been implemented and carried out peacefully, but it has itself greatly contributed to creating a lasting peace among a multitude of peoples who had previously continuously slaughtered each other in wars over ethnic differences, territorial disputes, religious conflicts, and so on.

The EU is not a sovereign entity (yet). It is a confederation of sovereign states with an obvious drive toward consolidation. Nations enter voluntarily on the assumption that they will retain their sovereignty. And as soon as that is no longer the case, they may have to fight to leave.

Beyond that, what has the EU done to promote "lasting peace"? It is not a sovereign entity. It does not have an army of its own. It actually has no power to prevent European nations from going to war against each other. Furthermore, NATO would do nothing to prevent its members from going to war against each other, as Greece and Turkey are well aware. So why has there not been a major war in the center of Europe since the Second World War? Largely, because there is a broad consensus, among elites and masses alike, that such a war is undesirable.

If, however, the EU can be shown to have contributed to peace, it has done so *not* as a sovereign entity, but as a confederation of sovereign European states. I welcome such news, because as an ethnonationalist, I am all for a confederation of sovereign European states that promotes conflict resolution among its members and a common defense of the continent. But to create such a confederation, the issue of sovereignty must be clearly settled, not fudged with a "federal" compromise.

Counter-Currents, January 20, 2023

ONE WHITE STATE OR MANY?

This is my opening statement in a debate on "Ethnonationalism vs. Imperialism" with Gregory Hood on June 10, 2023. Hood's opening statement, which followed, can be found at *Counter-Currents*.[1]

By my count, there are 52 historically white sovereign states in the world today.[2] That's not a lot. That's one for every card in a standard deck. By "historically white," I mean a state that had a white majority and white culture within the last 70 years, during which plunging white fertility rates and non-white immigration began changing historically white lands into multicultural, multiracial dystopias.

Note that I am simply talking about existing white "states" or "countries." I will not talk about "nation-states" or "ethnostates," because most existing white states don't meet that description. The Vatican, for instance, is not the homeland of a people but the sovereign headquarters of a church. But this is the world we live in, so this is where we must begin.

---

[1] Gregory Hood, "The Empire is Inevitable," *Counter-Currents*, June 20, 2023.

[2] In alphabetical order: Albania, Andorra, Argentina, Australia, Austria, Belarus, Belgium, Bosnia, Bulgaria, Canada, Croatia, Cuba, Cypress, Czech Republic, Denmark, Estonia, Finland, France, Germany, Greece, Hungary, Iceland, Ireland, Italy, Latvia, Lichtenstein, Lithuania, Luxembourg, Macedonia, Malta, Moldova, Monaco, Montenegro, Netherlands, New Zealand, Norway, Poland, Portugal, Romania, Russia, San Marino, Serbia, Slovakia, Slovenia, Spain, Sweden, Switzerland, Ukraine, Uruguay, United Kingdom, United States, Vatican City.

In every one of these states, white birthrates are below replacement. If these trends persist, the white race will become extinct, even in the absence of non-white immigration, which is at alarming levels in most historically white countries.

How, then, can we save the white race? We need to play our cards right. We have been dealt 52 sovereign states. Sovereignty means a state controls its own internal affairs. A sovereign state is empowered to say "no" to all subsidiary jurisdictions. A sovereign state also has the power to say "no" to other sovereign states and to transnational bodies like the UN, the EU, and NATO. Sovereign states can control their own borders. They also have the power to create incentives and remove disincentives to healthy population growth.

Thus if whites around the world are to be saved, our goal should be to take power in as many historically white sovereign states as possible, preferably all of them. Then we need to use state power to raise white birthrates, end non-white immigration, and begin non-white emigration.

The wild card is the Vatican, which is untroubled by low birthrates among its celibate residents. Nor is it beset with immigrants. But the Vatican could still do a great deal to combat the demographic decline of white Catholics.

It sounds like a huge task for a small movement. But you shouldn't wonder if a small but organized and fanatical minority can change the course of history, because they do so all the time. Truth be told, they are the only force that makes history. They always have. So how do we begin?

First, we need to spread the word about white demographic decline, its causes, and its cures. Then we need to find courageous and farsighted people in every white state to create white preservationist movements. These movements need to raise public awareness of anti-white demographic trends, propose workable solutions, and organize politically to contest for power on all levels of the system. But the ultimate goal of our movement should be to gain the highest levels of power in as many sovereign states as possible, then implement the necessary policies to save our people.

Who is most likely to support such efforts in the white states that exist today? They will tend to be people with strong attachments to their own kith and kin, including their own ethnic group. They will tend to have pro-natal, pro-family values. They are likely to be patriotic, ethnocentric, and even nationalistic. But they won't fall for the fake civic nationalism that declares Africans with a Swedish passport to be Swedes. They know that every real Swede is a white person, although they also know that not every white person is a Swede. They will tend to be on the political Right. Because they are attached to their own homelands and serious about connecting with and converting their own people, they will tend to look to their own traditions for models of the movements, policies, and champions necessary to save their countries.

But that doesn't mean that each of the 52 white preservationist movements must go it alone. Since all white lands face the same challenges and the same enemies, white advocates everywhere are more likely to triumph if they can cooperate with one another. They can share ideas, strategies, and tactics. They can support one another in international bodies. They can provide moral and material support to beleaguered comrades in other countries. Thus we need to maximize communication, cooperation, and solidarity among pro-whites worldwide. The more that we cooperate, the greater the chance that at least some white countries can be saved.

How can we maximize cooperation among pro-white movements? If two states wish to cooperate, they have to treat one another with mutual respect, meaning that they recognize the legitimacy of one another's sovereignty and interests. What is true of cooperation between states is true of cooperation between nationalist movements, nationalists being those most likely to insist on respecting the sovereignty of their own homelands.

What is the quickest way to chill international cooperation among white advocates? To reject the sovereignty of any white state. Again, the people who are most likely to promote white survival in any particular state are also the most likely to be fervent patriots and nationalists. Attacking the sovereignty of a white state thus makes enemies of those who were most likely to be our friends, i.e., those who were most likely to cooperate with and strengthen us in the most important struggle in the world against overwhelming odds and diabolical enemies. I can't think of a more self-defeating tactic if one's aim is to foster worldwide cooperation among white preservationists.

There are two principal ways to reject the sovereignty of other white states.

The first is the bad old zero-sum nationalism of the past, in which nations struggled to preserve their own sovereignty while denying the sovereignty of their neighbors. They refused to treat others as they wished to be treated themselves. I hesitate to even call this position nationalism, since there is a better word for when one nation aggresses against another. We call that imperialism. I wish to reserve the word "nationalism" for the good kind of nationalists, who believe in nationalism for all nations. They treat other peoples as they would like to be treated themselves.

White preservationists don't have the power to launch wars against other white states. But every white nation has historical grievances against other white nations due to the bad old nationalism. Oftentimes, it is possible to chill international cooperation between pro-white groups simply by rehashing old wars and old grievances.

Morally speaking, this is even worse than the bad old nationalists, who may have been evil, but at least they weren't stupid. At least they believed they were gaining some tangible benefit by attacking their neighbors. But nobody benefits when white preservationists fall out over battles that took place in the past rather than pull together to fight the great battle of our time.

The second way to sabotage international cooperation is the idea of one great white state: a white imperium or "civilization-state." I have criticized the principal arguments for one big white state in my essay "Against Imperialism," and we shall surely revisit them in the course of this debate. But before we go into such arguments, let's take a step back and ask ourselves how such discussions will impact our current struggle.

In today's 52 historically white sovereign states, I know of pro-white individuals or groups in 44 of them. I don't know of any in Moldova, Kosovo, Cyprus, San Marino, Lichtenstein, Andorra, Monaco, or the Vatican. But maybe I haven't looked hard enough. I also know of white preservationists in majority non-white countries like Chile and Brazil.

All of these individuals and groups feel strong attachments to their families, their homelands, and their race. Many of them struggle daily with alienation, demoralization, and oppression. But the strongest prevail. They talk to family, friends, even complete strangers. They post ideas online. They form virtual and real-world networks. They found webzines, publishing houses, active clubs, and activist groups. Some of these groups grow into political parties. Some of these parties actually win elections. A few actually govern.

But all of these institutions, large or small, began with small, individual acts of courage in particular places and at particular times. Someday, I would like to see a worldwide congress of white advocates from all 52 states, as well as white minority populations around the world. I would like to see them all working together for the preservation of our race. But that dream will only emerge from the grassroots efforts of white advocates in their own countries.

What's the last thing these people need to hear from us? How about that their efforts are "petty." That they live in silly little "comic opera" states that don't really have sovereignty. That their efforts are doomed to defeat. That their peoples and cultures have no future except as provinces of one great white state. But not to worry, they will be granted "autonomy" by the capital to speak their quaint languages and dance their quaint dances on their little Estonian and Slovenian and Hungarian reservations. So they should stop working to take state power in their own countries and wait for an emperor to save them.

If I were crafting propaganda to demoralize white activists, I couldn't come up with a better message.

Personally, I think we should encourage grassroots white preservationist efforts in as many countries as possible, not pour cold water on them. But the "one white state" idea is a great gush of cold water, delivered from on high. Even if one white state were supported by strong arguments (which it is not), I want to argue that it is impolitic, bad optics, even bad taste to bring it up, because it denigrates the grassroots efforts of pro-whites around the world.

Ethnic nationalist movements, including separatist movements such as in Flanders, are where the energy and numbers are. Aside from a few would-be emperors, there isn't much of a constituency for one big white state.

Fortunately, from my experience in the quaint, comic opera statelets of Europe, the idea of one white state has had little negative effect, largely because it is dismissed.

It is seen as an "American" idea, because most Europeans don't recognize Americans as a distinct people, compounded out of other peoples. They see us as simply generic, deracinated whites hankering for a generic white state. I have criticized this false image of Americans in my essay "American Ethnic Identity,"[3] where I argue that Americans are a distinct white people who deserve a homeland of their own.

There are no generic white people. There are many white peoples distinguished by their languages, cultures, and histories. Thus White Nationalism does not mean one homeland for one white people. It means many homelands for many white peoples. White Nationalism in America is American nationalism. Just as White Nationalism in Spain is Spanish nationalism.

The idea of one big white state is also seen as apologetics for the bad old imperialist "nationalism." Yockey's *Imperium* was a defense of Hitler's imperialism. Yockey's *The Enemy of Europe* was a serpentine defense of Stalin's. Today's Eurasianists are simply dismissed as apologists for Russian/neo-Soviet imperial revanchism, which is in fact true.

Today's Europe consists of the shattered remnants of old empires. Today's Europe is in the pincers of American and Russian imperialism. Europe also faces an enemy within: the EU, which even now gnaws at its entrails. Given this history—given this present situation—I think we can understand why European nationalists want to preserve and perfect their sovereignty, not throw it all away.

But don't nations and national identities change over time? Couldn't whites grow out of their particular identities into a pan-white identity? Couldn't they become like Americans, a new people compounded out of many different peoples? Yes, of course, today's distinct white nations could disappear. Countless peoples throughout his-

---

[3] Greg Johnson, "American Ethnic Identity," in *In Defense of Prejudice*.

tory have disappeared not just by slaughter but by assimilation.

But how does that sound to the people whose grassroots efforts we wish to encourage today? Nobody wants to hear that his identity does not matter. Nobody wants to hear that he is regarded merely as fungible raw material for someone else's grandiose dream. That sounds like the globalist dystopia we all want to reject, just a smaller, whiter version of it. It does not sound like the respect that is the bedrock of productive collaboration.

America was founded by people who were willing to give up their homelands over religion, ideology, and money. The people who remained behind were not willing to do that. Moreover, the passionate identitarians among them are the least receptive to such a proposal. And those are precisely the people we need to work with.

Why do I oppose one white state? Because I think the idea harms rather than helps the cause of white survival. We have been dealt 52 sovereign historically white entities. That's where white preservationism must begin. That's where it has begun. That's where the energy is. That's where the people are. It seems mad to throw it all away to chase a meme. If we are going to save our race, we will save it one white state at a time.

Counter-Currents, June 19, 2023

Reply to Gregory Hood

This statement was written after my debate with Gregory Hood on "Ethnonationalism vs. Imperialism." It incorporates the substance of my extemporaneous response to his opening statement as well as my subsequent thoughts on his response to my opening statement.

Dear Kevin,

I decided to collect into a single document my responses to your debate statement[1] together with some afterthoughts and treatments of issues we did not have time to deal with during the debate itself. Since I was addressing you directly in the debate, I decided to preserve that mode of address in a letter.

My first thought about your opening statement was, "Wow. That's very eloquent and well-delivered."

But I found your ideas themselves unconvincing. You have very effectively summarized how badly things are stacked against us. You laid it on thick. But you don't offer any real solutions. In fact, your solution is so removed from present-day reality that it can only discourage grassroots pro-white efforts in white countries around the world.

A Contradiction in Your Position

We disagree on several important philosophical points. But before I dig into them, I want to point out a contradiction in your argument.

---

[1] Gregory Hood, "The Empire is Inevitable," *Counter-Currents*, June 20, 2023.

You haven't really offered an argument for one white state. Instead, you've basically offered an argument against organizing pro-white movements in any other place but America—and presumably also Russia, although such organizing would get you promptly gulaged—on the grounds that smaller white states can't say "no" to America.

When asked where you think a white state is most likely to emerge, your answer was "America." But you haven't given us any reason to think that pro-white politics will fare better in America than in other white countries.

Won't the US government say "no" to pro-white communities in America too? Indeed, won't it be easier for the US government to quash any such movement within its own borders and under its own jurisdiction—as opposed to outside its borders, under the jurisdiction of another sovereign state?

I know that you think that sovereignty reduces simply to power, which means only big states are sovereign. But if national sovereignty means nothing in the face of an American veto, then lesser jurisdictions within America mean less than nothing.

You put a great emphasis on local community building. But if nation states can't stand up to the US government, then neither can the Wolves of Vinland.

The only pro-white community that could not be vetoed by the US government would have to either control or abolish the US government. Or, alternatively, control or abolish the American media, to which you sometimes ascribe sovereign power.

I think you need to explain how you envision going from grassroots community building to that level of power. And if it is possible in the US, why is it not possible in other historically white and putatively sovereign states?

Are you simply working on the assumption that

someday the US government won't be around to say "no"? In the long run, that's a reasonable assumption, since all things must pass. But then why shouldn't nationalists in other white countries organize based on the same hope?

The basic message you have for pro-whites outside of America is "Your enemies won't let you win." That's pretty much the definition of defeatism. Enemies seldom *let* you win anything. But we're not asking their permission. We simply must beat them.

Why do you think that your enemies will let you win in America? If you think they can be beaten, how? And if they can be beaten in America, somehow, why can't they be beaten in Europe or the Southern Hemisphere, which are further away?

Is America the Problem?

I also disagree that America is the central locus of the problem. Before Brexit, many Britons believed that the source of their ills was in Brussels. Since Brexit, the same problems have persisted because Briton is ruled by globalists as well.

Indeed, practically every historically white state is ruled by its own globalists. In Western Europe, a great number of these globalists regard the United States as retrograde and reactionary. They feel that the US is holding them back.

This is why sovereign states don't exert their power to say "no" to the US. It is not because they lack such power, but because they too are ruled by globalists who don't fundamentally disagree with America's establishment and even wish it were more radically globalist.

The issue is less the *political* hegemony of the United States but rather the *intellectual* hegemony of globalist ideas. If the US collapsed tomorrow, globalists would still be in control in most white states. Indeed, some of them would feel liberated.

Given that fact, I think it would be good for globalist elites to face grassroots nationalist challenges in all 52 historically white sovereign states. To raise up those challengers, we must sow the dragon's teeth of ethnonationalist ideas. As always, the intellectual challenge must come first.

You mentioned the pride flag. Does that fly around the world because America mandates it? Or does it fly around the world because there are homosexuals in every country who argue for it based on the same Left-liberal premises?

The pride flag is a symbol. Let's talk about something more substantive: the legalization of gay marriage, which is now policy in 35 countries, 27 of them historically white. Was this mandated by the United States? No, not even close. It was first legalized in the US in subsidiary jurisdictions in 2004—after the Netherlands, Belgium, and Canada. It became national policy in the US only in 2015—after the Netherlands, Belgium, Canada, Spain, South Africa, Norway, Sweden, Portugal, Iceland, Argentina, Brazil, France, Uruguay, New Zealand, and Luxembourg. As with the pride flag, gay marriage spreads because the same conclusions are drawn from the same premises which have been widely adopted around the world.

Why did Donald Trump lead the charge to legalize homosexuality in Africa? Why did alleged conservatives like Charlie Kirk applaud such efforts? Because conservatives think people are more important than principles, and they are addicted to "owning the libs" by out-libbing them. They are too timid, or too superficial, or too dumb, to challenge the hegemony of liberal ideas. But, as I have argued elsewhere, "Principles are More Important than People."[2] They are also more important than regimes,

---

[2] Greg Johnson, "Principles are More Important than Peo-

even the American regime.

THE PROBLEM WITH CONSERVATIVES

You are right that the conservative Victor Orbán banned the 2014 National Policy Institute conference in Budapest, and that the conservative government of Poland banned Jared Taylor from the Schengen Zone, twice.

But I am still right that the primary constituency for white identitarian politics around the world consists of people on the Right.

As for conservative politicians and pundits, even the good ones, they aren't really on our side. Many in our camp think that these people actually share our views, but they are just too cowardly to stand up for whites. After all, there are plenty of people in our camp like that.

But the deeper reason conservative types are our enemies, and always fail to protect their homelands, is intellectual. Conservatives accept—and we reject—the absurd idea that identity politics for whites, and only whites, is the worst possible thing in the world. It is the sin of "racism," which is only a sin when practiced by whites.

Who on earth thinks that white identity politics is the worst thing in the world? Jews, mainly. When conservatives like Tucker Carlson argue that the Left needs to step back from identity politics, lest white identity politics be awakened—when conservatives say that they are the last line of defense against white identity politics, they are not speaking to blacks or mestizos. They are speaking to powerful Jews. They are arguing that they, not the Left, are the most reliable servants of Jewish interests. It would be nice if conservatives cared as much about the ethnic interests of their own people as they care about the ethnic interests of Jews. But they don't, so

---

ple," in *The Year America Died* (San Francisco: Counter-Currents, 2021).

we will have to change their minds.

Once again, the primary enemy is a bad idea that has enthralled conservatives around the world. If America disappeared tomorrow, this idea would still control minds and policy in white countries. How do we replace this bad idea with better ones? I think that we must fight it everywhere it has taken root, in the context of whatever languages, cultures, and political systems that prevail there. That means that we must encourage rather than discourage grass-roots white activism in all white countries.

THE POWER OF IDEAS

How do powerless people challenge the powerful, especially when armed with mere ideas? If you think we need power to start with—if you think that only power can challenge power (as James Burnham says)—then the situation is hopeless.

I believe that power rests on legitimacy, not the reverse. The powerful can't rule by brute force alone. They need consent, and for consent, they need the imprimatur of moral legitimacy. Thus the powerless can overcome the powerful by challenging and impeaching their moral legitimacy.

This is why they spend so much time burnishing their moral credentials and blackening ours. This is why we spend so much time decrying the lies, follies, coverups, double standards, and other moral outrages of the establishment.

The less legitimacy the system enjoys, the less consent they enjoy, the less power they have, the more they must resort to naked coercion. But coercion further erodes legitimacy, which can lead to a self-reinforcing downward spiral toward collapse. This is how the wagging finger of moralism can overthrow the most powerful states.

The same is true of the media. Their power rests not

on technology, monopoly power, and censorship. It rests on their credibility. It rests on people's willingness to take them seriously. Their credibility, however, is collapsing, and our efforts have a great deal to do with that, even though we have a tiny fraction of their money and personnel and operate from the margins of society.

WHAT IS SOVEREIGNTY?

If sovereignty simply reduces to power, then no one has sovereignty. If France is not sovereign because the US is more powerful, then the US is not sovereign, because the US is not more powerful than an alliance of the rest of the world against it. Thus the equation of sovereignty and power is reduced to absurdity.

What is sovereignty? It is a moral norm. It is analogous to the rights of individuals. Under international law, a sovereign state bears certain rights that are recognized by other sovereign states. Sovereign states control their own internal affairs. They have the power to say "no" to all lesser internal jurisdictions. They have the power to say "no" to other sovereign states. Sovereign states, large and small, have equal rights under international law, just as individuals big and small have equal rights. Sovereignty does not make a state autarkic or invulnerable, just as rights don't make individuals bulletproof. But when a state's sovereignty has been violated, it has been wronged, and it—and other states—are entitled to bring the aggressor to heel and to justice.

Do such norms matter? Yes, because no matter how cynical politicians are, they still at least pay lip service to them. No nation, not even the most powerful, can afford to dispense with them altogether, because no nation has the power to resist the whole globe in a game of pure power politics. Hobbes was right. If you are serious about power politics and take it to its ultimate extreme, you will be forced to take refuge in moral norms.

ETHNONATIONALISM AS A RIGHT
You write:

> . . . concerning the idea of ethnonationalism. Where does it start? Every people gets their own nation. Okay, well, does Cornwall get to secede? Does Wales? Does Northumbria? These are all secessionist movements that really exist.

Ethnonationalism is the idea of a world order in which every people that aspires to independence has the right to a sovereign state of its own. To that end, ethnonationalists support the rights of secession and irredentism, i.e., the rights of the same people, separated by artificial borders, to join together in a larger state. We also support the idea of population transfers to decrease diversity and increase homogeneity in regions troubled by multiculturalism.

When should this happen? Simply when there are two or more peoples sharing the same state? Not necessarily. Some peoples may be content with the current situation. For instance, the Romansch people of Switzerland have not had any significant agitation for independence since the nineteenth century, probably because they do not feel their language and identity to be threatened in the Swiss Federation.

For new ethnostates to be born, there must be (1) a people with a distinct sense of identity that (2) believes that its existence as a people is threatened by the current order and (3) believes that it would be better off under a different state. In those circumstances, a people should be able to exercise their right to exit and either join another state or form their own state.

Why should other states care about this? Ultimately, because blood will be spilled. Multiculturalism promotes conflict and the destruction of cultural and biological diversity, and the most elegant solution is to separate warring tribes into different sovereign nations.

Ethnonationalism should be seen as a *right*, not a *duty*. You are *obligated* to do your duty. You have the *option* of exercising your rights. The Cornish and Northumbrians are not *obligated* to have their own states. Is there even a Northumbrian people today? Or is it just an administrative division of England?

But if the Welsh or the Cornish feel that their existence as peoples is threatened by remaining in the UK, then they should have the right to exit, and no force on earth should have the right to oppose them. Indeed, the international community should come together to support them and ensure that the process of redrawing boundaries and/or moving populations is orderly and humane, consistent with the basic human rights of all people involved.

STATES VS. NATIONS

You continue:

> But if you actually believe in your ethnic nation, at some point you're going to want to draw the line, because in any such order, the country that can prevent the most secessionist movements and control the most territory is going to be the strongest.
>
> You can say you want independence for your own nation, but if you're willing to let groups within that nation break away, especially in marginal cases where you don't have something like a 90% majority, I suggest you don't actually love your nation all that much. You don't want it to be powerful. You don't want it to be strong. So do you really want it? And what's the point of it?
>
> This is indeed the logic of empire. Your state becomes

stronger and richer by adding territories and peoples. It remains so by preventing peoples and territories from breaking away. Diversity, apparently, is a strength now.

I believe the opposite: Every nation is better off by increasing its homogeneity, even if that means letting go of subject peoples and territories. Unless, of course, you believe it is ethical for some states to reduce other peoples and their territories to simple repositories of natural and human resources. But if you believe that, on what grounds, exactly, do you object to what is happening to white peoples today?

WHAT KIND OF UNITY?

You write, "The West works best at a time of unity, from the Greeks fighting off the Persians to the Crusades." The Greeks fought the Persians and the Christians fought the Saracens as alliances of many different sovereign states. That's a far cry from a single sovereign entity. Advocates of one white state frequently claim that it is the only way for whites to survive great geopolitical conflicts. But this is simply not true. Military alliances of sovereign states are sufficient to meet any challenge.

THE NEW WHITE MAN

As an ethnonationalist, I believe in the one people, one state principle. You argue for one white state based on the fact that whites are becoming one people. Ethnic differences matter less and less due to globalization, and whites are attacked simply as whites.

But the erasure of cultural differences by globalization is largely superficial. Beyond that, the erasure of identity is nothing to embrace. It is just one more reason to fight against globalization. Moreover, the fact that our enemies see us merely as white is an error on their part, and it is certainly no argument for seeing ourselves simply as white.

I don't believe that generic white people exist. All white people also belong to particular ethnic groups. Europeans think that White Nationalism is an "American" idea because they think Americans are merely generic white people, created by blending deracinated white stocks. I have argued against this view in my article "American Ethnic Identity."[3] Americans are a distinct people and as such require our own homeland. White nationalism does not mean one nation for generic white people, but many nations for many distinct white peoples.

Why talk about biological whiteness at all? Because biological whiteness sets the outermost boundaries for assimilation into a white nation. Logicians make a distinction between *necessary* and *sufficient* conditions. Contra civic nationalists, biological whiteness is a *necessary* condition for being a member of any white people. A Somali with a French passport is not French. But biological whiteness is not a *sufficient* condition for being a member of any white people, because peoplehood requires a shared language and culture. Thus every Frenchman is white, but not all whites are Frenchmen.

I think it is possible to love yourself, love your family, love your community, love your city, love your culture, love your language, love your nation, and love your race. All these attachments are real. They radiate outward in concentric circles. They can also be balanced with one another.

But if all you care about is biological whiteness, that induces a kind of blindness. Replacement migration into a white country suddenly becomes fine if all the replacers are white. The destruction of white cultures and nations doesn't matter, because at the end of the process we still

---

[3] Greg Johnson, "American Ethnic Identity," in *In Defense of Prejudice*.

have whites. Even white extinction can be soft-pedalled because in 200 years, there will still be Amish, and they are white, right? Frankly, it would be a tragedy if whites became one white people for one white state. But the tragedy would be invisible if all you notice is that the end products of homogenization have white skins.

THE NEW WHITE STATESMAN

I believe that the one white state you advocate depends upon a new kind of man who doesn't exist. But I must lay my cards on the table. My position requires a new kind of statesmen in every white nation, and they don't exist either. Indeed, it requires a new model of international relations.

The ethnonationalist vision is of a new world order in which every people that aspires to independence has a sovereign homeland of its own. These ethnostates will live in peace because they will repudiate the bad old zero-sum, "beggar thy neighbor" nationalism, which I call imperialism. Instead, they will treat other nations as they would like to be treated themselves. They will respect one another's sovereignty and interests as a necessary condition of peaceful trade and cooperation.

The states of the world have always lived in a state of anarchy *vis-à-vis* one another. But history shows that anarchy isn't always chaos. There can be order without a common government. We owe it to ourselves to explore how this is possible. In international law, one finds the concept of the "comity of nations," meaning the mutual recognition of independent sovereignties. It is a form of collegiality, in which independent agents work together for common goals without an overarching political command structure.

My vision is a world in which a college of white ethnostates follows certain basic rules.

- ❖ First, no fighting amongst one another. This could be enforced by the other states agreeing to come to the aid of any white state attacked by another.
- ❖ Second, no alliances with nonwhites against fellow whites, which could be enforced in the same way.
- ❖ Third, no importation of non-whites into historically white territories.
- ❖ Fourth, no more white altruism to the rest of the globe. Trade yes, altruism no.

That's a lot to ask for. It requires a change of consciousness in every existing white state. Hence the need for grassroots movements in every white state. But this has always been an intellectual battle first and foremost.

Moreover, I think such statesmen are more likely to emerge than the new generic white man. If you are Czech, it is possible to think of yourself as Czech first, because that's most authentic. But it is also possible to have a broader civilizational and racial consciousness on top of that. That's what we need to work towards, as the crowning achievement of grassroots white preservationist movements around the world.

Counter-Currents, June 23, 2023

Russia & Ukraine, Again

This was my opening statement in a live debate on Odysee on March 26, 2022, on the topic "Nationalists in the West should support Ukraine against Russia in the current war." I argued the affirmative and Dr. E. Michael Jones argued the negative. I wish to thank Fróði Midjord of Guide to Kulchur for hosting this debate.

Nationalists in the West should support Ukraine against Russia in the current war. We need to distinguish two kinds of support: moral support and material support.

The case for moral support is simple.

As a nationalist, I support a world order of sovereign nations. Sovereign nations don't answer to other nations. That's what it means to be sovereign. Ideally, sovereign nations answer only to their own people. Sovereign nations have the right to differ with their neighbors. Sovereign nations have the right to choose their own friends and their own enemies. Russia wishes to deny Ukraine the right to align itself with Europe and America by launching a war. For nationalists, that crosses a moral line. From a simple nationalist point of view, Ukraine was operating within her rights as a sovereign nation, and Russia is violating those rights. Thus, nationalists of all nations should support Ukraine over Russia in the current war.

I am not just a nationalist; I am an ethnonationalist. Ethnonationalists think the best nation-states are *ethnically* homogeneous, because when multiple peoples live in the same country, under the same state, conflicts are bound to ensue. This is true even of peoples that are genetically and culturally very similar, like Ukrainians and Russians. For instance, some Russians under Ukrainian rule claim that they are being oppressed and that they can't be themselves. Well, if it is bad for Russians to live under Ukrainian rule, it must be equally bad for Ukrainians to live under Russian rule. If Ukrainians are better off ruling themselves in their own homeland, then the Russian invasion of Ukraine is obviously a bad thing. Thus, ethnonationalists should support Ukraine over Russia in the current war.

Like most modern states, present-day Ukraine is not ethnically homogeneous. Although the population is overwhelmingly ethnically Ukrainian, it is divided between Ukrainian-speaking Ukrainians and Russian-speaking Ukrainians. There are also Russians in the east, Hungarians in the west, Poles in the north, Bulgarians and Greeks in the south, and other minority groups.

The official language of Ukraine is Ukrainian, and Ukrainians require members of linguistic minority groups to learn Ukrainian in school so they can communicate with their fellow citizens and participate in civic life. Ukraine does not prohibit them from speaking their native tongues. Indeed, such policies are repulsive to Ukrainians, because under both the Tsars and Bolsheviks, the Ukrainian language was repressed by the state, which is why so many Ukrainians now speak Russian as their first language.

Even though Russians are not the only minority in Ukraine, only Russians have demanded that their language have official parity with Ukrainian. To the average Ukrainian, this is outrageous. White Americans would be similarly outraged if entitled minorities were to demand that Spanish or Ebonics have official parity with English in the United States.

It is not unreasonable for citizens of Ukraine to learn the Ukrainian language. It is not oppression to require it. If ethnic Russians feel oppressed, it is only because they have a misplaced sense of entitlement. They resent the fact that *their kind doesn't run Ukraine anymore.* The government no longer caters to foreign minorities. (Or at least not the Russian minority. As in Russia and the rest of the white world, Jews are a foreign minority that enjoys immense privileges. They aren't arrogant enough, however, to demand that Hebrew have parity with Ukrainian.)

Not catering to the Russian sense of entitlement falls far short of any reasonable standard of oppression. And if minorities in Ukraine really feel oppressed, most of them have homelands they can move to where their language is predominant: Russia for the Russians, Hungary for the Hungarians, etc. Most Russians in Ukraine stay because they don't feel oppressed, because they are attached to where they were born, and because they don't wish to be ruled by Moscow.

However, unlike Ukraine's Russian minority, Ukrainians don't have another homeland they can move to. Ukraine is their only homeland, and now it is under assault by Russia. Thus, as a Western nationalist, I give unqualified moral support to Ukraine in the current war.

There is, however, a danger in declaring moral support for Ukraine. We must mind the difference between moral support and moral hysteria. We cannot let moral support spiral into self-righteous Western virtue-signaling, with a concomitant demonization of Russia and Putin.

This war must end someday, the sooner the better. The best way to end it is a negotiated settlement. But it is hard to negotiate if one has to climb off one's moral high horse to make a deal with someone you have painted as the devil. You may think that Putin is evil, stupid, and dishonorable to start this war. But we must hope that he is also good, intelligent, and honorable enough to sign a peace treaty.

What about material support? Nationalists in the West should give material support to Ukraine in this conflict, but with some serious qualifications.

First, it is appropriate for Western individuals, organizations, and governments to give money and other forms of support to Ukrainian refugees. This duty falls heaviest on the nations bordering Ukraine: Poland, Slovakia, Hungary, Romania, and Moldova. This is required by simple moral reciprocity. Misfortune can befall any nation, and someday the citizens of those countries might be forced to take refuge in Ukraine.

Second, it is appropriate for Western individuals, organizations, and governments to economically boycott and sanction Russia and Russian individuals with strong ties to the Russian regime. Nobody is morally obligated to trade with Russia. Boycotts and sanctions weaken and internally divide the Russian regime, impeding its ability to wage war.

But there are significant qualifications here. It is stupid to boycott Russian artists like Anna Netrebko or Valery Gergiev, or to extort political statements out of them. It is even stupider to "cancel" Tchaikovsky or Dostoevsky. Short of an actual war, it is both criminal and stupid to seize Russian state and individual assets, and such actions actually risk escalating into a war. Similarly, there is an immense moral and practical difference between a boycott and a blockade. For one, a blockade is an act of war.

Third, if Ukraine is to remain a sovereign homeland for the Ukrainian people, it must put up a respectable resistance to the Russian invasion. Thus it is appropriate for the West to give Ukraine military aid: arms, training, and intelligence.

But let's be careful here. The United States followed the path of economic sanctions and military aid into two world wars. We can't afford a Third World War, because Russia is a nuclear power, which means it would be the Last World War. Thus, it is appropriate to offer material support for Ukraine, as long as it does not lead to a wider war involving NATO and the United States.

Russia's rationale for this invasion is fourfold.

First and foremost, Putin does not want Ukraine to join NATO. But since sovereign nations have the right to choose their own friends and enemies, Putin's invasion to abrogate that right is simply wrong. Now, cynics and "realists" like to say that bullying small countries is just what Great Powers do, and it isn't prudent to try to stop them, because they are powerful, and we might get hurt. But surely political realism also recognizes that small nations seek allies to protect themselves from big nations, which is why Ukraine wanted to join NATO. If realism counsels tolerance of great powers bullying small countries, then surely it counsels tolerance of small countries seeking allies against great powers. If you recommend we tolerate Russian aggression but not Ukrainian attempts to enter NATO, you're not a realist. You're just a shill for Russia.

Russia's invasion is not an argument against joining NATO. It is only an argument against *failing* to join NATO, since it would not have been prudent for Putin to attack a NATO country, because he might get hurt. If Putin thought this war would reduce the number of NATO countries on Russia's borders, he was sorely mistaken. For one, if Russia conquers Ukraine, she will thereby border on four NATO countries: Poland, Slovakia, Hungary, and Romania. Second, because of this war, NATO is much more popular in Europe, and even formerly neutral nations like Sweden and Finland are talking about joining.

Russia also offers three more or less throwaway arguments for this war: that Ukraine is oppressing Russians in the East, that Ukraine is a fake nation, and that Ukraine is full of "Nazis."

Requiring Russians to learn Ukrainian in school is hardly oppression, nor is saying "no" to the demand for Russian linguistic parity. Since 2014, Ukraine has been fighting against two Russian-backed separatist "people's republics" in the East: Donetsk and Luhansk. This is hardly oppression either, because the Russians started these conflicts and could switch them off at will. Russia demands that Ukraine recognize its breakaway client states. I think that Ukraine would be better off simply ceding these territories, along with Crimea, which Russia seized in 2014. It might help end the war, and it would leave Ukraine smaller but more ethnically homogeneous.

Ukrainians reject this idea. First, they don't think giving up territory would bring lasting peace. They believe the Russians would simply invent new pretexts for further incursions into Ukraine. Second, they regard Donetsk and Luhansk as fake Russian ops that do not represent the actual interests or popular will of the Russian minority. Many ethnic Russians are fighting against Russian-backed separatists and Russian invaders alike. Not all ethnic Russians want to be ruled by Moscow. Nevertheless, I think Ukraine may be forced to cede these territories. If it brings even a temporary end to hostilities, it would be worth it.

The charges that Ukraine is a fake nation and that it is full of "Nazis" are far more ominous.

The relationship of Russia to Ukraine is analogous to the relationship between the United States and England. They are distinct nations with many similarities and long stretches of shared history. Just as America is an offshoot of England, Russia is an offshoot of Ukraine. If one studies American history long enough, eventually it becomes English history. One cannot understand Jamestown and Plymouth without looking at English history. One cannot understand religion in America without studying the Reformation in England. One cannot understand American law and government without looking at English law and government. The same is true of Russia and Ukraine. For instance, one can't understand the origins of Russian Orthodoxy without reading about Grand Duke Vladimir of Kyiv. But both America and Russia evolved into distinct nations over time.

Thus, if Americans were to suddenly declare that "England is a fake country," that its apparent cultural differences are merely a form of false consciousness, that the English drive on the wrong side of the road merely to spite Americans, and that England should be ruled from Washington DC, it would sound quite insane.

It sounds equally insane when Russians say Ukraine is a fake country. But that did not stop Vladimir Putin from saying it. Nor does it stop millions of Russians from believing it. A good thing about national sovereignty is that it protects us from being ruled by foreigners with crazy ideas. But now Ukrainian sovereignty is under Russian assault.

If Ukrainians are a fake people, then their language, culture, and national self-consciousness—anything that differentiates them from the Russians, really—are simply what Marxists call "false consciousness," that can be dislodged by "reeducation," which is a Marxist euphemism for brainwashing and terror. If Ukrainians are a fake people who are "really no different" from Russians, they have no right to a sovereign homeland. Once the Ukrainians are stripped of their homeland by war and their national self-consciousness through reeducation, those who survive will be assimilated into Russia. Ukraine and Ukrainians will simply disappear from the pages of history. This is genocide by any reasonable definition, and genocide is wrong.

When Putin vows to "de-Nazify" Ukraine, he's not just talking about the Azov Battalion. He's not just spreading boob bait for Russian octogenarians who think the Second World War is still on. He's not just trolling the Western media. Under Communism, Russians had a long history of declaring their enemies—indeed, entire peoples—as reactionary, fascist, or Nazi. Putin is using "Nazi" in exactly the same way that Jews use it in the West: as a slur against the nationalism and patriotism of other nations. It is a slur against what Putin calls "cave-man nationalism," i.e., ethnic nationalism. De-Nazifying Ukraine thus means destroying the national self-consciousness of the Ukrainians, which stands in the way of their conquest and assimilation by Russia. Thus "de-Nazifying" Ukraine is just another euphemism for cultural genocide.

But surely Putin's Russia is not the same as the Communist Soviet Union. Some things, obviously, have changed. But Putin is a product of the USSR. He was an agent of the KGB. He mourns the downfall of the USSR, defends and conceals Communist crimes, treats Communist propaganda as fact, and employs Communist techniques of propaganda and subversion, many of them directed at the nationalist and populist Right in the West. Ukrainians who remember how Moscow brought them oppression, famine, and terror have every right to fear and prepare for the worst.

In sum, nationalists in the West should offer unqualified moral support for Ukraine as a victim of military aggression and a target of cultural genocide. We should offer qualified material support— economic boycotts and sanctions, and humanitarian and military aid—that stops short of widening the war. Finally, Western nationalists should support a negotiated peace as soon as Russia is convinced that it cannot impose its will through military conquest.

Counter-Currents, March 29, 2022

What's Really at Stake in Ukraine

In my debate with E. Michael Jones on the Ukraine War, my opening statement argued that nationalists in the West—and indeed, around the world—should support Ukraine against its invader, Russia. E. Michael Jones argued that Westerners should not support Ukraine.

Jones began with the history of Jews in Ukraine, apparently assuming that if Jews are involved with anything, it can't be good. Then he argued that the war is really not between Russia and Ukraine but between Russia and America. There wasn't a lot of substance to his argument, so I will address it only in passing while dealing with bigger issues.

I will grant that Jews are overrepresented in positions of power in Ukraine and the West, but they are also overrepresented in such positions in Russia. Thus there are Jews on both sides of this war, so no matter which side you take, you are going to end up agreeing with some Jews. Thus this war cannot be seen simply as Jews vs. non-Jews. You can't explain the differences between two parties in terms of what they have in common. This war is about another, more fundamental clash between Russia and Ukraine that has polarized the Jewish community as well.

Is this an ethnic war between Ukrainians and Russians?

Ethnicity certainly plays a large role in the enmity between ordinary Ukrainians and Russians. But this explanation is not sufficient either. The focus of the war has now shifted to East Ukraine, which has large ethnic Russian minorities, and where Russia and two breakaway puppet states, the Donetsk and Luhansk "People's republics," have been fighting Ukrainian forces since 2014.

But there, at the heart of the war, the conflict is not simply between Ukrainians and Russians. It is also between Russians and Russians. Ethnic Russians in the Donbas region are fighting against ethnic Russian separatists in Donetsk and Luhansk, who are aided by Russians from Russia as well as foreign antifa and Communists, some from the Third World. These separatist states are Russian military operations, controlled by Moscow. If Kyiv granted their independence today, they would be applying for union with Moscow tomorrow.

Furthermore, Russians from Russia herself have come to Ukraine to fight against Russia.

Why are Russians fighting Russians in Donbas? Why do Russians in Donbas not wish to be ruled by Moscow? The answer is complex. Based on conversations I had with Russians in Ukraine, both when I visited Ukraine in 2018 and later, by means of the Internet, three reasons stand out.

First, some Russians see this as a war against Communism, plain and simple: the Communism of the Donetsk and Luhansk People's republics and their foreign antifa fighters. They associate Communism with terror, death, and rule by scum. They don't wish to submit to that.

This might not be the most sophisticated understanding of what is going on in Donbas. If you tell them that Putin is really behind the breakaway republics, they will simply tell you that KGB alumnus Putin is a Bolshevik as well. They don't care if people are hoisting the Soviet flag out of nostalgia, irony, or red-brown fusionism. They think people who fly that flag and carry arms against them deserve to die.

Russian anti-Communists in Ukraine mock Western ethnonationalists who suggest that they should cede sovereignty to Communists on ethnonationalist principles, as if Communists are setting up ethnostates and wish to grant equal rights to Ukrainians to have their own state. Besides, where would that leave Russians who don't want to be ruled by Moscow?

Second, some Russians are fighting alongside Ukrainians against Moscow and its proxies because they regard Ukraine as the cradle of their civilization, much as Americans, Canadians, and other Anglosphere-dwellers regard England and the broader United Kingdom. Just as Rightist Americans like T. S. Eliot were attracted to England because they felt that America was a fallen civilization—fallen away from important things still preserved at its source—some Russians are attracted to Ukraine. Many Russians who come to Ukraine in particular reject the Byzantine and Mongol-influenced despotism associated with Moscow for the more egalitarian, free-spirited, nationalistic—and Western—political traditions associated with the Kievan Rus and later the Cossack hosts. Ukraine, whatever its faults, is a freer and more Western country than Russia, and some Russians gravitate toward that, seeing it as a part of their own heritage that has been lost in Russia.

Third, Russian ethnonationalists have taken refuge in Ukraine because they are persecuted in Russia. Putin's Russia is a multiracial, multicultural empire, with an aggressively multicultural ideology. Russia is ruled by a small oligarchy that is visibly less ethnically Russian than the Russian Federation as a whole. It is worth looking at the "early life" sections of Russia's richest men: Jews, part-Jews, Uzbeks, Muslims from the Caucasus, Ukrainians, Byelorussians, and other non-Russian ethnic groups are all overrepresented. It is surprisingly difficult to find information on the ethnicity of Putin's cabinet ministers (or their wives), but Defense Minister Sergei Shoigu is half-Tuvan/half-Ukrainian, Foreign Minister Sergey Lavrov is half-Armenian/half-Russian, and former Transport Minister Igor Levitin is a Jew from Ukraine. If Russia put Russians first, this elite's power and wealth would be threatened. Thus, just as in the West, the Russian oligarchy pushes multiculturalism and suppresses Russian ethnonationalism.

When Russian ethnonationalists complain that Russian birthrates are below replacement, whereas indigenous Mongoloid and Muslim populations are rising, the elites feel threatened. They don't care about Russian ethnic interests. They care about maintaining peace among the different peoples of their empire.

When Russian ethnonationalists complain about being displaced by Muslim immigrants from the post-Soviet "Stans," the elites feel threatened. Like Western elites, Russia's rulers feel more secure if they can dilute the Russian majority with outsiders.

Russian ethnonationalists complain that the Russian military is increasingly reliant on non-Russians—Mongoloids and Muslims—who create ethnic mafias in the military and prey upon ethnic Russians. These troops are also more likely to commit war crimes than Russian troops (handy, if you treat war crimes as a tool of policy).

Russia's rulers, however, have always recruited non-Russians for their military: under the Tsars, under the Soviets, and after the Soviets. This is an old tool of imperial statecraft. One creates an empire by sending one's own people to die conquering other peoples. Obviously, rulers who do that can't have a deep attachment to their own countrymen to begin with. One holds onto an empire by using conquered peoples to garrison other parts of the empire, including the "homeland," since soldiers are more willing to kill people who don't belong to their own ethnic group.

Empires also promote outsiders into their ruling elites. Thus Russia's rulers have never been all that Russian, even under the Tsars, when the elites interbred with Mongols and then Germans. Bolshevism changed the ruling elite, filling it with peoples conquered by the Tsars: Jews, Georgians, Poles, Latvians, Ukrainians, and so on, as well as ethnic Russian Bolsheviks. But this new elite still feared the ethnic Russian majority and continued to play the old games of imperial statecraft to keep them subjugated. Even today, Russia's multiethnic rulers are more afraid of ethnic Russians than they are afraid of Muslims and Mongoloids, so they don't see an increasingly non-Russian military as a problem.

Russia's military is just as wedded to "diversity, equity, and inclusion" propaganda as the Western military. Nationalists argue that this weakens the military. This is true, if one thinks of the military as primarily a tool to fight foreign wars. It is false, if one thinks a white military is a threat to the power of the elites and a diverse military is a handy tool to suppress the white majority. Our rulers and the Kremlin's are united on this point.

This is why the oft-cited comparison of Russian and American military recruitment videos is laughable. The Russian video features a tough, masculine white guy (who is reportedly a gay porn actor). This is contrasted with an American video about a female soldier with two mommies. Of course, the comparison is highly misleading, since American military recruiters also appeal to macho white guys (and prepare them for the Great Replacement), and Russians have their own repulsive diversity propaganda. The lesson we are supposed to draw is that our diverse army could never defeat an army of tough Russian white guys. The truth—as we have seen on the battlefield in Ukraine—is that the Russian army is not all that tough, not all that Russian, and not all that white. Russia's army is as diverse and weak as America's.

Diversity definitely is a weakness during war. But most of the time we are at peace, and during peace, imperial elites regard diverse armies as less threatening to their power than homogeneous ones.

Putin's Russia, like America, is a multicultural, multiracial empire ruled by a rootless, sociopathic, and disproportionately alien elite that uses multicultural propaganda and race replacement as tools to suppress the white ethnic majority. Following the Jewish template, Putin stigmatizes all forms of ethnic nationalism as "Nazism" and uses the holocaust as a tool of anti-nationalist, pro-multiculturalist indoctrination.

In America, ethnonationalists are primarily being censored and deplatformed by private corporations. Such harassment is inconvenient, but not insuperable. In Putin's Russia, however, ethnonationalists face harsh repression and extrajudicial murder. This is why many Russian ethnonationalists chose exile in Ukraine and are now fighting against Putin's multiracial invaders.

If Russians and Ukrainians are fighting side-by-side against Moscow, this is not primarily an ethnic struggle. What, then, is the deep issue that unites Russians and Ukrainians against Moscow? *The real issue is imperialism versus nationalism.* Russian ethnonationalists, like Ukrainian ethnonationalists, don't want to live under Moscow's multicultural, multiracial, ethnocidal regime.

Russian ethnonationalists agree with the Russians who look to Ukraine and the West as a freer alternative to Russia's Byzantine-Mongol despotism, but *their deeper concern is that the Russian imperial machine is inimical to the very existence of the Russian people*, expending their lives in imperial wars then using subject peoples to tyrannize over and ethnically displace them.

Even though Russia shed vast numbers of non-white subjects after the collapse of the Soviet Union and the secession of the various Stans, there are millions of non-Russians within Russia's borders. Russians are about 80% of the current population, but their birthrates are below replacement, while the birthrates of non-Russians—most of them non-whites or Muslims—are above replacement. *Russian ethnic decline is thus built into the current system, even without non-white immigration, which is also flowing in from the Stans.* Beyond that, if the Eurasiansists have their way, Russia may well reabsorb some of the Stans. They are already pursuing extensive economic integration with Central and East Asia. None of this bodes well for ethnic Russians. Imagine what America would be like today if China, not Mexico, were on its southern border.

Russian ethnonationalists also agree with the anti-Communist Russians who took up arms against the separatists in Donetsk and Luhansk, but they think there is a deeper problem here than just the Communist ideology of the breakaway republics and their foreign fighters. Donetsk and Luhansk are simply Russian imperial operations. Their appeals to Marxism are just tools of Russian imperialism. The real enemy is the Russian imperialist mentality and machine, which are far older than Marxism and the USSR.

Although Putin follows the Jewish playbook of stigmatizing all forms of ethnonationalism as "Nazism," some of the Russian ethnonationalists in Ukraine to whom I have talked really are National Socialists. It seems odd for Russians and Ukrainians to be attracted to National Socialism, given that Hitler aimed to reduce their peoples to helots and colonize their lands with Germans. But they reject Hitler's petty chauvinism out of a sense of racial and civilizational brotherhood. They also typically bond over Black Metal music and mixed martial arts. Like ethnonationalists all over Europe, they are both committed to their own homelands and cultures and also feel deeply connected to our common race and civilization. These nationalists, both Russian and Ukrainian alike, don't regard ethnic Russians as such as their enemies. Their enemy is Russia's multicultural ruling elite and its imperialist mentality. This is a far more nuanced outlook than that of the average Russian or Ukrainian man in the street, who at this point hate one another intensely and regard "no more brothers' wars" moralizing as daft. It sounds paradoxical, but Russian and Ukrainian neo-Nazis are far more capable of living and working together than Russian and Ukrainian normies.

The Ukraine War is a conflict between Russia, a multiracial empire with an aggressive multicultural ideology, and Ukraine, the homeland of the Ukrainian people. This conflict, in one form or another, has existed since the seventeenth century. It has existed longer than the United States, and it would exist even if the United States were completely uninvolved. It is far older than NATO, and it would exist even if NATO were not involved. It would even exist if Jews were not involved. All these other parties are merely accidental, incidental, and along for the ride. If the United States, NATO, and the European Union were not offering aid to Ukraine, the Ukrainians would simply have courted other allies—because the real issue here is the old struggle between Russian imperialism and Ukrainian nationalism.

Imperial Russia has not just started a war against Ukraine. Russia has also vowed to "de-Nazify" Ukraine, which means destroying its national self-consciousness—basically anything that would prevent the Ukrainians who survive from being assimilated by Russia and disappearing from the pages of history. This is simply cultural genocide.

If you are fine with this because you think that Putin is conservative, Christian, reactionary, or illiberal, then you are not a nationalist who puts the preservation of our race and its distinct peoples above all else. Please come clean about this. Then let's shake hands and part ways here.

In the war between imperial Russia and Ukraine, there's only one side that genuine ethnonationalists—even Russian ethnonationalists—can support: Ukraine.

Because this conclusion is so blindingly obvious, Russia's apologists try to reframe this conflict entirely. They claim that Russia is not fighting an imperial war of aggression against Ukraine. Instead, she is fighting a war of self-defense against America, which is "the real imperialist."

Counter-Currents, April 9, 2022

The Ukraine War, One Last Time

This is my opening statement in my debate with Mark Collett on the Ukraine War hosted by Joel Davis on YouTube on Saturday, October 15th, 2022. I got cut off at the end. The last three paragraphs were written for the very end of the debate, but by then the format had broken down, and there was no way to get them in.

I want to thank Joel for hosting and moderating, and Mark Collett for joining me in what I would like to describe as a civil airing of differences on the Ukraine War.

The first question we need to ask is: Why are White Nationalists commenting on this war in the first place? I am under no illusions that my opinions on this war, one way or another, will have any effect whatsoever on the consequences. So why talk about it at all?

Because even if my commentary will have no short-term effect on the war, I am playing a much longer game. I am an advocate for White Nationalism. As I define it, White Nationalism is a species of ethnonationalism, the view that the best world order consists of sovereign nation-states for all peoples who aspire to them.

Ethnonationalism is the best global order for two principal reasons: First, it respects the differences between peoples and races and secures their own spaces in which they can live according to their own identities; second, multiracial, multicultural empires are cauldrons of ethnic strife, hatred, and the erasure of identity. By separating warring tribes into their own homelands, ethnonationalism promotes peace.

Ethnonationalism is opposed to imperialism in all its forms. Imperialism is a form of multiculturalism, in which different peoples are subject to a single political order, which again encourages hatred, conflicts, and cultural destruction. Ethnonationalists do not, however, oppose trade and cooperation between sovereign states, including the creation of customs unions to facilitate commerce and defensive pacts to deter aggression.

The main reason I comment on the Ukraine War is to show the relevance of the White Ethnonationalist idea. Russia is the world's largest land empire, and it used to be much larger, embracing Finland, the Baltic states, Poland, Belarus, Ukraine, Moldova, the Caucasus, and the Central Asian Stans. After the Second World War, it ruled the Warsaw Pact nations as well. After the collapse of Communism, these nations gained their independence.

Post-Communist Russia is an obscenely rapacious oligarchy ruled largely by former Communists, including state security agents like Putin, tyrannizing over a profoundly degraded and demoralized populace with astonishingly high rates of alcoholism, drug abuse, divorce, abortion, HIV infection, and domestic violence. Imagine an America where, outside of New York and Los Angeles, everything else consists of West Virginia and Indian reservations.

Russia's ruling elite openly mourns the collapse of the Soviet Empire and dreams of putting it back together. Russia fought two bloody wars against Chechens who were trying to gain their independence. Russia uses ethnic Russian minorities in neighboring states as fifth columnists and pretexts for interventions. Russia has fomented Russian riots in the Baltic states. Russia has fomented secessionist and irredentist wars in the Caucasus, Moldova, and Ukraine. About the only former imperial possession Russia has not meddled in is Belarus, a wholly subservient satellite state.

After the collapse of Communism, Ukraine had a referendum on independence. Every single region voted for independence from Moscow. In 1994, Russia and the United States were parties to the Budapest Memorandum, which recognized Ukraine's 1991 borders in exchange for nuclear disarmament.

Despite this, Russia has worked for decades to turn Ukraine into a Belarus-style satellite. Ukraine overwhelmingly favored pursuing European Union membership. In 2013, Russia tried to prevent this with economic sanctions. Then Putin simply bought Ukraine's President, Viktor Yanukovich, who abruptly reversed course on EU membership, which sparked the Maidan revolution, a glorious outburst of Ukrainian national populism which Russia slanders as an American intelligence operation. Meanwhile, Russia launched its own military and intelligence ops in Ukraine, seizing control of Crimea and fomenting separatist movements in the Donbas. Now, eight years later, Russia has invaded Ukraine with the express aim of "regime change" and "de-Nazification."

Ukraine, Russians claim, is a fake country. Ukrainians think they are a different people, but this is false consciousness, which they must be educated out of by destroying their language and national identity. This is a war of imperial conquest, pure and simple. Its frank aim is cultural genocide. Its pretexts—the Donbas "genocide," NATO encroachment—are transparently cynical and not to be taken seriously.

If you believe that distinct peoples deserve their own homelands, if you believe that wars of conquest and cultural genocide are evil things, then of course you should sympathize with Ukraine over Russia.

But again, our sympathies are not going to change this war one way or another. The only reason I comment on it at all is to uphold the correct ethnonationalist principles and show their relevance, because I hope that in the very long run, if we can get enough people of vision and good will on our side, ethnonationalism might create a better world, free from horrors like the Ukraine War.

I do, however, wish to make one brief nod to *Realpolitik*, specifically with regard to the White Nationalist movement itself, because in this context, the things I say actually can make an immediate difference.

Vladimir Putin is very bad for White Nationalism: in Russia, in Ukraine, and in the West. After taking power, Putin passed sweeping anti-"hate" legislation, which was used to target not just outright National Socialists but milquetoast immigration reformers. Putin also set up a fake nationalist movement, Nashi, that combines the usual raft of conservative cultural values with Russian imperialism, which is a multicultural ideology opposed in principle to all forms of ethnic nationalism.

Putin's fake Russian nationalist movement has aggressively courted nationalists in the West. I remember in 2014, when Leonid Savin, one of Alexander Dugin's followers, submitted an article on "Donbas Ethnonationalism" to *Counter-Currents*. I was offended. Did he really think I was that stupid? I remember a conversation with a Eurasianist who said that suitcases of Russian and Iranian cash could appear if one gave platforms to their propaganda. I was pretty sure he was dreaming.

Beyond that, you can't get to an ethnonationalist world if you are suddenly willing to shill for Russian imperialism and anti-nationalism. Today our movement's only advantages are the truth and the credibility one wins by speaking it. Compromising one's principles and credibility for . . . what, exactly? . . . is simply self-defeating. But, given the behavior of some nationalists in the US and Europe, I suspect they were taken in.

This is a battle I can fight and win, which is why *Counter-Currents* has taken a leading role in combatting the Russian subversion of the White Nationalist movement since 2014.

As a White Nationalist, my worst nightmare would be

a Donald Trump dictatorship. Why? Because Trump is committed to a multicultural, multiracial, civic nationalist vision of America. Given that, even if he built a wall, the white race in America would be relentlessly eroded by differential fertility, miscegenation, and *legal* immigration—and under a Trump dictatorship, there would be no way to change it. Trump would turn countless potential Right-wing dissidents into plan trusters, who would embrace and make excuses for white genocide as long as Trump appealed to their conservative values and authoritarian personalities. Imagine the fate of Kevin MacDonald under the dictatorship of the man who pardoned Jonathan Pollard. Imagine the fate of Jared Taylor under the dictatorship of the man who gave us criminal justice reform and proposed the Platinum Plan.

That nightmare is reality under Putin's dictatorship today. That nightmare is what he wishes to impose on Ukraine, which has one of the largest, best-organized, most radical, and most righteous White Nationalist movements in the world today. To that, I hope every principled White Nationalist will join me in saying: Hell, no. That's no way to run a world.

How to end this war? If there were justice, Russia would go back to its 2013 borders, pay reparations, and put Putin's head on a spike on the Kremlin wall. Sadly, there won't be justice. There will just be a negotiated settlement. But there won't be a negotiated settlement until Putin is beaten on the battlefield. So first military aid, then diplomacy.

If the negotiations were conducted according to ethnonationalist principles, then the ethnic strife in the East would be terminated in two ways: moving borders and moving people. There should be fair referendums voted on solely by people who occupied the disputed territories in 2013. The 2014 Crimea referendum and the recent referenda in the east, conducted after ethnic cleansing and under military occupation, are insulting farces. The result of fair referenda would probably be Crimea staying with Russia and Russian separatists in the Donbas migrating to Russia.

Of course, Ukrainians would not trust Russia to keep any such agreement, and for good reason. They didn't honor the Budapest Memorandum, after all. But Russia probably would respect Ukraine's borders if she became a member of NATO or an equivalent mutual defense pact. Indeed, this war never would have happened if Ukraine were a member of NATO.

Counter-Currents, October 17, 2022

Questions on NATO, Russia, & Ukraine

This is the second part of my Ukraine War debate with Mark Collett on October 15, 2022. After our opening statements, the format was to answer questions posed by the host/moderator Joel Davis. These are my answers to the first five questions. I appended my answer to the sixth and final question to my opening statement.

1. Was Russia justified in invading Ukraine? What responsibility does NATO have in creating the Ukraine crisis?

Russia's invasion is pure imperialism. I would say naked imperialism, were it not for the tiny fig leaves of the "genocide" in Donbas and NATO encroachment.

I do think the US was stringing Zelenskyy along with the possibility of NATO membership to bait Putin into this war. I think the US had a very clear idea of how corrupt the Putin regime is and how weak the Russian military proved to be. I think they believe that a defeat for Putin could bring about regime change. I think that Putin was a fool to start this war. But baited or not, he was still the one to start it.

On a deeper level, though, NATO has no real responsibility for this war for the simple reason that Ukraine joining NATO was a disposable pretext. If NATO had given Zelensky a hard "no," Putin would have invented another pretext, because I think he was hellbent on seizing Ukraine and thought it would be easy.

There's a lot of disinformation about NATO in Russian propaganda.

NATO made no promise to Gorbachev not to expand

eastward. They did promise not to put nuclear weapons in East Germany, a promise they kept. NATO expanded to the east because the countries there had legitimate security concerns *vis-à-vis* Russia. Unlike the Russian Empire or the Soviet bloc, NATO did not expand by conquest. NATO is a defensive alliance that countries ask to join.

Nor did NATO rebuff Russia. Putin asked why Russia was not invited into NATO. He was told that countries apply to join, and the members vote on it. Putin said that Russia would not wait in line behind insignificant countries, and that was the end of it.

Putin's attitude, of course, was pure Russian chauvinism. Under international law, all sovereign states are equal, hence equal treatment by NATO. Putin, however, thinks that you are only as sovereign as you are powerful. He does not fundamentally respect the sovereignty of smaller nations, which is why Russia's former satellites wanted into NATO in the first place.

NATO's member states are not "vassals" of America. What would happen if a NATO country tried to leave? Would there be regime change? Did America attack France in 1959 when she withdrew her Mediterranean naval fleet from NATO command? Did America attack when France refused to permit foreign nuclear weapons on its territory, forcing 200 US military aircraft out of France? Was France attacked in 1963 for withdrawing its Atlantic and Channel fleets from NATO command? Were there American tanks in the streets of Paris, as there were Soviet tanks in the streets of Budapest in 1956 and Prague in 1968? No, the other members of NATO respected France's sovereign decisions.

Nor does NATO threaten Russia. NATO is a defensive alliance. It would not go to war with Russia unless Russia attacked one of its members. NATO, of course, has been used beyond its remit, for instance in Serbia and Libya.

But that won't happen to Russia because she has an enormous nuclear deterrent.

The idea that Russia cannot live behind its 2013 borders is nutty, yet we are told that this is an "existential" conflict. But the only thing existentially threatened by staying within its borders is Russia's imperialist mentality.

NATO was built to contain Soviet imperialism. When the USSR was dissolved, it looked like NATO was obsolete. That impression was wrong. Russia's post-Communist regime mourned the loss of their empire and immediately set to work subverting the newly-independent nations—which is why 15 of them applied to join NATO.

The only reason Ukraine was invaded is because it was not in NATO and did not enjoy its protection. This is why Sweden and Finland have now joined NATO. Armenia and Georgia should join as well. Putin's war has strengthened NATO enormously.

2. What attitude should nationalists in the Anglosphere have towards NATO? Is NATO an anti-white geopolitical force?

Let's not limit this to the Anglosphere. As a White Nationalist, I believe in white solidarity. When a white nation is attacked by a multiracial empire, I believe in coming to its defense. I think it is blatantly immoral to argue that we should be indifferent to the fate of other white nations because, somehow, the destruction of Ukraine would make it easier for us to fix our own governments at home. Even if that were true, it is at best petty nationalism, not White Nationalism.

If I believe in white solidarity, then I should also want organizations in place to defend white nations from aggressors. NATO happens to be performing that role right now, so I am happy with that.

Is NATO an anti-white geopolitical force as such?

When NATO was founded, most of its signatories were deeply racist nations. The United States had immigration policies committed to maintaining a white supermajority. It had segregation in the South. It was a genuine white supremacist society. Germany based citizenship on German blood. NATO did not change all these things. The changes moved through different channels entirely. As my friend James A. argued recently in a piece I reprinted at *Counter-Currents*, NATO has not wrecked Poland, and not being in NATO has not saved Ireland.[1]

Even though many NATO countries have insanely anti-white regimes, with the arguable exception of Turkey, NATO is an alliance of white nations that are committed to mutual defense if any member is attacked. That makes NATO a *de facto* pro-white alliance, regardless of the politics of people like Biden or Macron.

3. Is the Russian Federation anti-white? Is the Russian Federation a threat to pro-white politics in Eastern Europe (and beyond)?

Yes, absolutely.

Russia is a multiracial empire in which the white majority has below replacement fertility, and the only growing populations are Chechens and Tuvans. Russia also has large numbers of non-white immigrants from the Stans who are more fertile than Russians. As White Nationalists, we all know what those trends mean in our own countries. They mean the same thing in Russia: Unless these trends change, in a couple of centuries the average Russian will be a Muslim with significant Mongoloid DNA. The only way to preserve the Russian people is to create a Russian ethnostate.

In the West, we are more or less free to advocate for

---

[1] James A., "The Intermarium Alliance," *Counter-Currents*, July 26, 2022.

ethnonationalism. We can even advocate ethnonationalism for Russians. But in Russia, that will get you gulaged as an advocate of what Putin calls "cave-man" nationalism. Russia is an authoritarian society with aggressively pro-multicultural, anti-nationalist propaganda—and short of revolution, there's no way to change it. This makes Putin's regime bad for whites in Russia—as bad as a Trump dictatorship would be for whites in America.

Putin's express aim in invading Ukraine is de-Nazification, which does not refer simply to Azov. Russians use "Nazi" and "fascist" like Jews do in the West: to stigmatize any patriotism, national identity, or national self-determination other than their own. Russia also brands Poland, Finland, the Baltic states, and now even Sweden as "Nazi."

Francis Parker Yockey described the Soviet Union as the leader of the outer revolt of the non-white world against the white world. Putin's speech of September 29, 2022, which so many in our movement have lauded, is direct from the Soviet anti-white playbook. As Michael Tracey asked on Twitter: "Who wrote this, Noam Chomsky?"

Finally, Putin's regime has made a concerted effort to subvert ethnonationalist movements in the West. He has Western ethnonationalists ready to drop their principles on the spot to shill for Russian geopolitical interests. Some of the marks of this shilling are:

- ❖ Selective anti-Semitism: Jews make America and Ukraine bad, but Putin can dedicate a monument to the Red Army in Israel with "an army of Jewish billionaires" at his side, and . . . no comment.[2]

---

[2] Gil Stern Shefler, "At Putin's side, an army of Jewish billionaires," *The Jerusalem Post*, June 26, 2012.

❖ Selective self-determination: Self-determination is good in Donbas and Crimea but bad for Ukrainians, Chechens, and the Baltic states, not to mention Kurds in Syria or Tibetans and Uighurs in China. Some empires are good, apparently, others are bad. (In the debate, Collett actually airily referred to Russian multiculturalism as "natural" because it is a big country [the word is "empire," and they are made, not grown], but he also referred to Ukraine as an "artificial" state whose Russian-made boundaries needed to be redrawn to reduce multiculturalism.)
❖ Selective anti-Islamism: Muslims in Ukraine can behave like Muslims in Rotherham and provoke no comment from some Western nationalists.
❖ Selective concern with demographic decline, differential fertility, and replacement migration. Western nationalists sound the alarm about the long-term consequences of such trends in their own homelands, but when confronted with the same trends in Russia, Russia's apologists in our ranks will suddenly revert to cuckservative arguments circa 1965, dismissing the very possibility of demographic change as alarmism.

Such contradictions don't help Russia, but they do undermine your credibility if you support them.

I don't know what the Russians or their Western supporters think they are getting out of this. I don't think our opinions will affect the outcome of this war one way or another. I suppose it is flattering that the Russians think we are important enough to subvert, but they are doing terrible damage to our movement for no measurable benefit to themselves.

I don't know what Western nationalists think they are gaining by supporting Russia. Some, surely, have fallen for a form of the QAnon delusion that they have powerful friends in high places. But we don't. We have to fight this regime ourselves. Some, surely, play too many video games, where they enjoy real dopamine from imaginary agency and imaginary victories. Time to put away childish things. Some, surely, are paid agents of influence, although it is reckless to make such accusations based solely on circumstantial evidence.

But the accusation of selling out for money is actually the most charitable, because although it is dishonorable, it is at least "rational" in some sense, whereas "selling out" for no apparent benefit at all is baffling.

My mind is drawn to the grotesque image of a huge cuckoo chick being frantically fed by tiny birds who have been fooled into thinking this monstrous parasite is their own offspring. Such cuckoldry is all too common among humans. It is easy for us to see when it takes the form of whites adopting non-white babies or opening their borders to non-white migrants because their natural nurturing instincts have been hijacked by anti-white propaganda.

We need to react with equal horror when we see mental cuckoldry in our own ranks. We are fighting the most evil establishment in history, with almost no resources but truth and courage. We can ill afford to pour our scarce credibility, time, and money into the bottomless gullet of Russian imperialism.

Our movement gets nothing from Russia apologetics, but it costs a great deal. In the short term, it causes polarization, ill will, and the breakdown of our ability to work together toward our true mission: saving our race. In the long run, it undermines our effectiveness as racial champions by making it unclear what we stand for. Championing contradictory ideas also undermines our credibility.

4. Does Ukraine's right to national sovereignty necessarily trump nationalist concerns with US/NATO power projection?

Whose nationalist concerns are you talking about? Are you talking about "geopolitics" here? Because when I hear that word, I reach for my pistol, because I sense I am about to hear that I can somehow advance White Nationalism by giving verbal assent on the Internet to something blatantly immoral, anti-white, and anti-nationalist.

Yes, Ukraine's national sovereignty trumps "geopolitical" concerns with US power projection, purely on principle, because the only geopolitics White Nationalists care about is creating a world of sovereign states.

But if such abstract principles leave you cold, still yes, because Ukraine is a very special country, where white ethnonationalism is very strong. Ukraine could be the first country in Europe to have a genuine ethnonationalist regime someday. If Ukraine became part of NATO and the European Union, it would be a natural ally of nations like Poland and Hungary against the worst influences of the West.

Russia's apologists love to say that if a country joins NATO or the EU, it will be flooded with non-whites and trannies. Ukraine, they say, would be doomed. Well, if it really is their position that countries like Ukraine or Poland or Hungary, with their large nationalist movements and stubbornly sensible populations, are doomed by NATO and the EU, what hope do Western nationalists have? If Svoboda and Azov and the National Corps can't beat back Western decadence, what chance has the National Justice Party? If Orbán can't win, then what chance does Patriotic Alternative have?

5. Can/should NATO be reformed? What would be the ideal Western security architecture?

I am a White Nationalist, which means I am a partisan of a political system that does not exist (yet), not a partisan of any existing political system. That said, from a White Nationalist point of view, some are better than others. Beyond that, I can understand why countries faced with the real-world choice between NATO membership or being a Belarus-style satellite of Russia are eager to join NATO, even though they are aware of all the problems with the West.

There are definitely bad things about NATO. NATO has encouraged the militaries and martial spirits of most of its members to atrophy. Finland and Sweden have excellent militaries and have a great deal to lose under NATO. Also, NATO has been used by the US as way to impose Jewish-penned free speech violations on new members. When Romania wanted to join NATO, for instance, they were told it was problematic to honor Marshal Antonescu. The United States would actually oppose the NATO membership of a country that adopted the US Bill of Rights. Obviously, those are bad things, but they are hardly the apocalyptic predictions of Russian propagandists, and nothing compared to the tyranny exercised within the Warsaw Pact and the USSR proper, which is the main reason those countries find NATO membership so desirable.

But, for all that, yes, NATO can be reformed. NATO would be great if every NATO member country had pro-white leaders. That is up to every nationalist movement in every NATO country to accomplish. Obviously, that's a long way off. And short of that, Central and Eastern Europe would probably be better off with the Intermarium alliance that has been widely discussed at *Counter-*

Currents since 2015.[3]

The Intermarium was an interwar Polish geopolitical idea to create a military alliance of nations between the Baltic and the Black Sea to serve as a cordon sanitaire, sealing off Europe from Russian Bolshevism. A modern Intermarium could embrace Finland, the Baltic states, Poland, Chechia, Slovakia, Hungary, Romania, Moldova, Ukraine, Bulgaria, and even the former Yugoslav republics. Together, these nations have the power to deter any Russian aggression short of nuclear warfare, but they would also protect the most racially and culturally healthy countries in Europe from Western decadence.

Southern Europe also needs a way to seal off the continent from Africa and the Near East.

Counter-Currents, October 18, 2022

---

[3] Beginning with Émile Durand, "Toward a Baltic-Black Sea Union: 'Intermarium' as a Viable Model for White Revival," *Counter-Currents*, October 19, 2015.

THE DUGIN ASSASSINATION

On August 20th, 2022, Darya Dugina, the daughter of Russian geopolitical thinker Alexander Dugin, was killed when her vehicle exploded as she was leaving a festival where her father spoke. The bomb was probably meant for her father, who was expected to depart in the same vehicle but apparently changed his mind at the last minute.

My first thought was that in Russia, some people take ideas very, very seriously. But in truth, Dugin was probably targeted because of his real or imagined role in Kremlin politics.

I have always been skeptical of Dugin. Based on his books *The Fourth Political Theory*[1] and *Heidegger: The Philosophy of Another Beginning*,[2] as well as his articles and interviews, I concluded that Dugin and I have read a lot of the same writers and detest many of the same things, but on the most essential points we have reached diametrically opposite conclusions. I am a White Nationalist. Dugin is anti-white[3] and anti-nationalist.[4] He is an advocate of Russian imperial revanchism and thus a cheerleader for Russia's invasion of Ukraine, which I oppose on ethnonationalist grounds. Ukraine is the homeland of the Ukrainian people, and Russia needs to stay out.

---

[1] See my satire on *The Fourth Political Theory*, "North Americanism: A Modest Proposal," in *Truth, Justice, & a Nice White Country*.

[2] Greg Johnson, "Dugin on Heidegger," in *Graduate School with Heidegger* (San Francisco: Counter-Currents, 2020).

[3] Giuliano Adriano Malvicini, "Dugin Contra Racism," *Counter-Currents*, September 11, 2014.

[4] Giuliano Adriano Malvicini, "Do Nationalists Need Dugin?," *Counter-Currents*, September 19, 2014.

I am also skeptical of Dugin's influence. He has been touted as the philosophical and geopolitical mastermind behind the Putin regime. Dugin has been called "Putin's brain" (as if Putin had no brain of his own) and "Putin's Rasputin" (as if Putin were pious and weak-minded). Dugin is definitely part of Russia's late Communist and post-Communist political establishment, but I suspect that his outsized reputation is largely his own creation, since it first issued from his various publishers and platforms, whereupon it was eagerly repeated both by those who wished to deify or diabolize him.

But there's no solid evidence that Dugin has any special influence on the Kremlin. Despite their extremism and esoteric embroideries, Dugin's ideas on geopolitics and Russian foreign policy are rather commonplace. Dugin occupies no prestigious positions. His primary patron is the oligarch Konstantin Malofeev. There's a real possibility, however, that he was targeted, and his daughter was killed, because of the mastermind reputation that he so carefully crafted.

One's reaction to the Dugin assassination depends, of course, on who did it. But we don't know who did it, and we may never know. There are plenty of suspects with means and motive, but they fall into three major categories. First, there are Dugin's rivals and enemies in the Russian establishment, including his own Eurasianist movement. Second, there are Dugin's enemies in Ukraine. Third, there are other foreign intelligence services.

The latter two options seem the least likely. It is expensive and risky to assassinate one's enemies on foreign soil, and if the Ukrainians or other foreign intelligence services were willing to undertake such an escalation, surely they could have found a more significant target than Dugin. Of course, they may have believed Dugin's own hype. But targeting cabinet ministers, military brass, or industrialists would inspire more fear and create more problems for the regime. Perhaps such people have better security than Dugin. But there may have been more tempting targets at the very festival Dugin was leaving. Thus it seems more likely that Dugin was targeted by domestic enemies, who would have had easier access to him. Dugin would seem like a small target for foreign actors, but he might loom much larger for people closer to home, especially rivals within his own camp.

Of course, mere ignorance of who perpetrated this crime won't stop people from commenting on it. Why let a spectacular murder go to waste? The Kremlin, predictably, has accused the Ukrainians. Dugin himself has accused them. Surely he believes this, since otherwise he would be a monster to exploit his own daughter's death for cheap political points. The Ukrainians, just as predictably, have blamed the Russians.

The reactions on the Internet fall into two broad camps: hopes and prayers vs. jeers and sneers. Generally speaking, the people who are mourning Darya Dugina are far from Russia and anti-Ukraine. Those who are celebrating her death tend to be closer to Russia and pro-Ukraine. I can't fault people who actually knew Darya Dugina from sharing their feelings. But when vast numbers of strangers chime in on either side, it is a tasteless spectacle of social signaling.

People who view Dugin and his daughter simply as intellectuals react to this assassination the same way that they reacted to the attempted assassination of Salman Rushdie: as an attempt to use brute force rather than reason to deal with intellectual opposition.

Those who view Dugin and his daughter as primarily political actors who have been cheerleaders for the Ukraine War have reacted much as Iraqis or anti-war Americans would react if Liz Cheney were blown up by a bomb meant for her father. The Dugins, both father and daughter, cheered on the deaths of countless Ukrainian fathers and daughters, so it is hardly surprising that some people return the sentiments.

What do I think of this assassination? It's complicated. It depends on who did it and why, which we will probably never know for sure. If Dugin was being targeted for his ideas, I am outraged, since I believe that intellectual disagreements should be settled by reason, not force. If Dugin was targeted as a political player by his fellow Russians, that's obviously no way to run a country, but it was a game that Dugin himself chose to play. If Dugin was targeted as a warmonger by Ukrainians or their allies, well, that's also part of war. Wars are no way to live with your neighbors, but that too was a game that Dugin chose to play, and his daughter chose to follow him. If this is too horrible for you to contemplate, don't blame the messenger. Blame the war. You are getting only a taste of the horrors that have been unleashed upon Ukraine for the last six months.

How should our movement handle this assassination? Those who knew the victim should have their say. But I wish the rest of us had maintained a dignified silence rather than exploit this event for novel "hot takes" or to launch embittered attacks on rival camps.

Personally, I think compassion rather than mockery is the proper response to this horror, although I understand those who prefer to save their compassion for the Ukrainians. As I put it in my essay on David Lynch's *The Elephant Man*:

> We are all curious about bad things that befall other human beings: accidents, illnesses, deformities. If we satisfy our curiosity, the result is horror. At this point, however, there are two basic ways to deal with horror: mockery or compassion.
>
> As Anthony M. Ludovici argued in *The Secret of*

Laughter, laughter is glorying in one's superior fitness. Forced or nervous laughter, however, is an attempt to reassure oneself that one really is more fit.

But the horror we feel is ultimately based on the recognition that misfortune can befall us all. . . . none of us is immune to misfortune of one sort or another. Compassion is the recognition of this fact: one sees oneself in the other and feels for him as one feels for oneself. Mockery is a lie and evasion, compassion an admission of the truth.[5]

Counter-Currents, August 24, 2022

---

[5] Trevor Lynch, "The Elephant Man," in *Trevor Lynch's Classics of Right-Wing Cinema,* ed. Greg Johnson (San Francisco: Counter-Currents, 2022).

NATIONALISM FOR ALL

Mike Maxwell of Imperium Press has written a thoughtful response to my position on the Ukraine War on the Imperium Press Substack account.[1] Maxwell thinks that it is appropriate for White Nationalists to support Russia's invasion of Ukraine because the Ukrainians are being supported by the United States and most other NATO members, so a defeat for Ukraine will be a defeat for our own governments, which will make our own work as dissidents easier. As he puts it, "quite clearly our highest national interests are served by the hostile ruling order at home getting its ass handed to it."

This argument is unconvincing for several reasons.

First of all, would Ukraine's defeat really be a serious blow to NATO and the United States? The US has survived a humiliating defeat in the Vietnam War. It has also bounced back from costly and embarrassing debacles like the Iraq and Afghan wars. So I see no reason to believe it would suffer a serious blow from a hypothetical Ukrainian defeat by Russia. The US and NATO are not even at war with Russia; they are merely aiding Ukraine. If the US can survive outright defeat in war, surely it can survive the defeat of an ally like Ukraine.

Second, let's just grant that Ukraine's defeat would somehow shake up the US in ways the Vietnam, Iraq, and Afghan wars did not. Would that still help dissidents? Exactly what are we being asked to imagine? The US government collapsing like the Soviet Union and David Duke becoming President? Based on what happened after the collapse of the USSR, in such a scenario we'd

---

[1] Imperium Press Substack, "Lemmy Nationalism," October 19, 2022.

more likely end up being ruled by someone like Merrick Garland or Michael Chertoff.

The Japanese attack on Pearl Harbor and the 9/11 terrorist attacks were humiliating defeats for the American regime. Did they help domestic dissidents? Absolutely not. Pearl Harbor was the pretext for a government crackdown on dissidents, and 9/11 was the pretext for the creation of an omnipresent surveillance state and the abandonment of significant due process rights. All we got was the right to say "I told you so" from the margins of society.

If the American regime experienced a Russian victory in Ukraine as a humiliating defeat, that could well become a pretext for further deplatforming and legal harassment of White Nationalists and others in the broader Right who have been cheering on Russia and amplifying Russian propaganda. And once such a process got started, we could only rely on our enemies' scruples not to deplatform and jail all the rest of us, for good measure.

For these reasons, I doubt that a Russian victory in Ukraine would benefit White Nationalists at all.

Beyond that, we need to take a step back from these arguments and reflect on this whole conversation. No matter which side we cheer on, White Nationalists are not going to affect the outcome of this war one way or another.

It is flattering that Russian propagandists have long tried to sway Western White Nationalists to their side, but frankly, they are deluded to think our opinions matter to this conflict at all.

White Nationalists who think they can affect the war are equally delusional, and they have less excuse. The idea that we can somehow increase our political clout by helping the Russian war effort by typing words on the Internet smacks of too many hours of online gaming. We are not statesmen, occupying a standpoint beyond good and evil, able to make Machiavellian bargains to throw our weight behind one of the parties in an actual war. This does not even rise to the level of LARPing, which, after all, means "live-action role-playing."

Moreover, the pro-Russia argument is not merely based on fanciful assumptions, it is also deeply immoral. We are being asked to cheer on a war of imperial conquest and cultural genocide launched by a Eurasian empire against a white nation, because that will somehow help us be nationalists in the West.

Even if that were true, what kind of nationalism would that be, exactly? It smacks of the bad nationalism of the past, in which European nations fought with one another and were even willing to ally themselves with non-Europeans to gain advantages over fellow Europeans.

One wonders how far these "nationalists" would go. If they are willing to cheer on the destruction of a European nation by a Eurasian empire, would they ally with China, Japan, the Muslim world, or India to the same end? At that point, it would be clear that white solidarity is simply a dead letter.

Maxwell recognizes that this is a problem, so he adds "No nation's interests are so important as to imperil the white race, but in practical terms no white nation's interests do imperil the white race, nor is this remotely likely ever to happen." In short, White Nationalists need not promote white solidarity and white preservationism as an alternative to the bad old nationalism, simply because such *Realpolitik* will never threaten the white race.

The bulk of Maxwell's article is an argument against "universal nationalism": the idea that the best world order is one of sovereign homelands for all peoples who aspire to self-rule:

. . . framing nationalism in universalist terms is a

dead end because nationalism is an inherently particularistic phenomenon. There's an ordinality to it that is lost when the abstraction nationalism is privileged above this nation here. . . . Nationalism is putting your nation first, and while there is nothing wrong with wanting to see other nations do the same, these can't both be the highest priority—you can't put your nation first while also putting the right of other nations to do the same first. They will invariably come into conflict, so which is it?

"Nationalism for all" is fine in the abstract, but we don't live in a world of abstractions, we live in a world of concrete nations, whose interests are zero-sum. There is nothing contradictory in me putting my family first, but there is something contradictory in me doing that while also defending my enemy's right to do the same.

Why can't you put your own interests first while recognizing that it is not just inevitable, but also right for other individuals, families, and nations to do the same? Let's say that ethnonationalists get the world we want. All empires are dismantled. Every people that aspires to autonomy has a homeland of its own. Is conflict in such a world inevitable?

No, not if all nations abide by the same rules, and rule-breakers are punished by other nations. What should the international rules of an ethnonationalist world order be? Simple: Each nation can put its interests first and allow other nations to do so as well by abandoning force and securing alliances and resources through voluntary, mutually beneficial exchanges.

This is a conversation that we should be having. We aren't statesmen yet. We are a tiny, marginal, powerless minority. Yet, we have made astonishing progress in injecting our ideas into the political mainstream, largely because we have the courage to speak forbidden truths to censorious elites.

But before White Nationalists get involved in politics, we need to do more than just complain about the status quo. We need to put forward a workable alternative, explain how we can get there from here, and create a movement to bring it about. That's why I discuss the Ukraine War. It is an opportunity to explain the real-world applicability of ethnonationalist principles. We have everything to gain by upholding these principles, and everything to lose by contradicting them to play-act as statesmen engaging in cynical *Realpolitik*.

Counter-Currents, October 27, 2022

MIGHT, RIGHT, & SOVEREIGNTY

One of the most common reasons people fail to communicate is that they use the same terms to mean different things. For instance, "bark" can refer to the voice of a dog or the skin of a tree, and a conversation between people who don't know they are using the term in two different ways is the stuff of comedy. In logic, we call this error "equivocation," meaning calling different things by the same name, and not knowing it.

The concept of "sovereignty" is often used equivocally, which causes immense confusion. The two senses of sovereignty that are most often conflated are: sovereignty as a *moral norm*, and sovereignty as *actual power*—sovereignty as *right* vs. sovereignty as *might*.

The confusion is multiplied by another distinction: *national* sovereignty vs. *popular* sovereignty. National sovereignty is the moral norm that nations don't answer to any higher political powers, but instead control their own affairs and do not meddle in other nations' internal affairs. Sovereign nations are also treated as equals under international law. Popular sovereignty is the norm that the good of the people is the state's highest law.

The most common objection to the norm of national sovereignty is that a nation is only as sovereign as it is powerful, meaning that only powerful nations are sovereign and weak nations have no real sovereignty at all. This implies that the equality of sovereign nations under international law is a mere fiction. It also implies that when a powerful nation invades a less powerful nation, it makes no sense to talk of a violation of sovereignty, because if a nation is weak enough to be invaded, by that very fact it has been proved to have no sovereignty.

Likewise, a common objection to the idea of popular

sovereignty is that the people do not rule. Instead, powerful elites rule. Again, sovereignty is reduced to power. Whoever has power over the state is sovereign, and if you are on the receiving end of state power, you are *ipso facto* not sovereign. Thus, it is meaningless to criticize any state for violating popular sovereignty. The very fact that popular sovereignty can be violated proves that it does not exist.

These arguments dismiss the very idea of norms. Moral norms do not *describe* what happens to be, i.e., the everyday world. They *prescribe* what *ought* to be. Morally speaking, the everyday world is a mixed bag: good, bad, indifferent. Moral norms are the standards by which we distinguish between the good, bad, and indifferent.

National sovereignty prescribes that sovereign states recognize and respect one another's autonomy. As far as this norm is concerned, it does not matter if one state is stronger than another. When one state violates the sovereignty of another, the aggressor is wrong, and the victim has been wronged. This moral outrage, moreover, is not altered if the aggressor gets away with it. Indeed, the longer it persists, the greater the outrage. Evils do not magically become goods with the passage of time. But some infamies can become so entrenched that nothing can be done to reverse them.

To preserve their sovereignty, states cannot set up a power above them that forces them all to get along, because if such a force existed, they would no longer be sovereign. One solution is for smaller states to band together to counterbalance the power of larger states. Another solution is to create international bodies like the United Nations or NATO to adjudicate disputes. But if these organizations are truly international—namely, relations between sovereign states—they cannot arrogate their member states' sovereignty. Thus, organizations like the UN and NATO are *collegial* rather than *political*. They are gatherings of independent agents working together for common aims under shared norms (international law), without an overarching power that commands them. Members of such organizations may elect leaders, delegate powers, and commission functionaries to carry out projects. But ultimate sovereignty is reserved by the member states.

Advocates of the norm of popular sovereignty recognize that all political orders require differences of power, and that power will always be exercised by the few over the many so that the rest of society can get on with their lives. The few rule, and the many are ruled. The norm of popular sovereignty prescribes that the ruling elite act in the interests of society as a whole (the common good) as opposed to their own factional interests. When rulers fail to pursue the common good, they are wrong, and the people are wronged. This moral outrage is not altered just because the elites might get away with it. Indeed, the longer they get away with it, the greater the outrage.

The denial of sovereignty's normative nature is a part of a broader denial of norms as such. Often, this view is expressed as "might makes right." But if right simply reduces to the power relations that exist at any given time—if whatever is, is "right"; or if we can never say that things *ought* to be different, even though we might prefer them to be—then we can dispense with concepts like the good and the right altogether and simply talk about facts.

If "right" is meaningless in politics, it doesn't just imply that weak people have no rights. It also implies that the strong have no rights. They do enjoy more power. But they should enjoy it while they can, because when somebody stronger comes along and takes it away, they have no grounds to complain.

This is a very strange doctrine for dissidents to embrace. Dissidents by definition oppose the existing power structure. That makes us weak by definition. We might *prefer* that the political *status quo* be different. But if it is meaningless for us to say that the system is *wrong* and *ought* to be different, why would anyone who does not share our preferences take them seriously? It is a trope in Western movies to point a gun at someone and declare, "You ain't talkin' yer way out of this." The truth is that, in such a situation, *all we can do is talk our way out of it*. In fact, one could describe the ideological component of metapolitics as *talking our way into power*, and nothing could be more self-defeating than declaring moral language meaningless before we start.

Fortunately, many of the "might makes right"/"right means nothing" crowd don't really mean it. They have a very specific picture of the "might" that makes right: the outstanding and splendid individual, the kingly type, the great lion. They are revolted when you point out the simple truth that great lions can be brought down by packs of jackals. You may be big and strong, but you've got to sleep sometime, and when you do, a bunch of skinny guys working together can end you. The mediocre masses banded together are stronger than the splendid few. But that's not the kind of power politics they have in mind. Thus they don't really believe that might is right. They believe in the inherent right of the *noble* to rule. But nobility is one of those pesky moral norms that they thought they had banished.

Counter-Currents, October 20, 2022

NOTES ON SOVEREIGNTY & INTERNATIONAL ORDER

Mike Maxwell has posed some questions to me on sovereignty and international order on the Imperium Press Substack.[1]

Ethnonationalists envision a world of sovereign homelands for all distinct peoples who aspire to autonomy. Thus we are opposed to multinational empires as well as global government schemes, all of which involve the denial of sovereignty to particular peoples or, in the case of global governance, to all peoples.

It is therefore fair to ask how an ethnonationalist world order would work. Would it be a world order or a world chaos?

Thomas Hobbes contrasted the state of nature, where there is no government, with civil society, in which there is government. In the state of nature, every man is sovereign, answering only to himself. But, Hobbes argued, life in the state of nature is a state of war of all against all, in which life is inevitably "solitary, poor, nasty, brutish, and short." Individuals in a state of nature would thus be driven by rational self-interest to set up a common ruler to create peace.

Hobbes' state of nature is not a description of how states actually form. Instead, it is a thought experiment showing that, in the absence of a state, rational self-interest would drive men to create one as soon as possible.

Hobbes did, however, point out that the different

---

[1] Imperium Press, "Populism or Vanguardism," November 1, 2022, https://imperiumpress.substack.com/p/populism-or-vanguardism

states of the world are in a state of nature in relation to each other, since there is no common power above them to enforce rules and secure peace.

Since ethnonationalists envision a world of 200-odd sovereign homelands, we need to explain why we do not follow Hobbes' reasoning to its logical conclusion: global government.

Is the life of nations in the state of nature as Hobbes described it, namely a perpetual war of all against all? Are the lives of nations in the state of nature solitary, poor, nasty, brutish, and short? Shouldn't nations prefer to surrender their sovereignty to a global government to ensure peace and prosperity? Isn't global government preferable to global anarchy?

War is one of mankind's greatest scourges. But in the state of nature, nations are not in a constant state of war of all against all. There are always wars somewhere, but even so, we observe peace almost everywhere else—peace without global government.

We also note that the lives of nations are seldom solitary. Every nation has some allies and trading partners.

Many nations in the state of nature are quite prosperous.

And the lives of most nations are hardly "nasty, brutish, and short." Indeed, some nations are breath-takingly civilized, refined, and ancient—and all in the state of nature that Hobbes claims we should flee as soon as there is an alternative.

How can peace and amity emerge among sovereign states in a state of nature, without a common power to enforce common rules? Sovereign states live at peace when they agree to respect one another's sovereignty. That means, in practice, that they secure alliances and resources through voluntary trade rather than violence. If all sovereign states foreswear violence and embrace mutual respect and voluntary interactions, there can be a global ethnonationalist order without a global state.

From an ethnonationalist point of view, therefore, an ideal world order is a form of liberalism without the state, known in some circles as "anarcho-capitalism." The only alternative to a global state is global anarchy. But, contra Hobbes, anarchy need not be chaos, for there can be order without the state.

In the absence of a common state, how can sovereign nations adjudicate disputes and deal with global problems like environmental degradation, international criminal and terrorist networks, or even planetary defense against comet or asteroid strikes like the one that ended the dinosaurs? By creating international treaty organizations to which they delegate powers to deal with particular problems while maintaining their sovereignty: organizations like the United Nations, for instance, which currently has 193 sovereign members.

Such organizations are not *political*, because there is no overarching power. Instead, they are *collegial*, meaning that they consist of independent agents united by common goals and shared rules, but not by a common power to which they surrender their sovereignty.

What happens in such a world if a nation goes rogue? Under international law, all sovereign states are equal. But some states are stronger than others. What if one wishes to gain by force what one cannot gain by negotiation? No state is so powerful that it cannot be opposed by alliances of smaller states. Such alliances could use moral suasion and economic pressures to bring rogue states back into the fold. But if peaceful measures fail, war still remains the last resort.

In short, such a system is not fool-proof or failure-proof. But it is better than any global government schemes, which promise to make such wars impossible—but only after, in effect, declaring war on and vanquishing (whether by stealth or open conflict) every state that wishes to maintain its sovereignty. Again, the only alternative to global government is global anarchy. Anarchy need not be chaos, but some chaos may still be preferable to global government.

Maxwell, however, apparently does not think there is an alternative to global or imperial government:

> . . . as for the rules-based order envisioned here, what gives the rules force? Who decides what rules? Who interprets? The subtext here is that we have something like the rule of law, on an international scale. . . . So, if we can envision a global patchwork of nation-states adhering to a set of rules, we must also envision an agent enforcing those rules. But why can't this agent be everyone? Can't all states check each other? Our first clue that they can't is that this is the same argument given by anarcho-capitalists, but on a smaller scale, for a stateless society. Robbing and cheating people will get you ostracized, and in a tiny village this may be enough for custom to prevail for a time. But before long, you'll need a council of elders, convened by one *primus inter pares*, and later formalized into a king. At anything much beyond the family (and maybe not even that far), you will end up with a state in embryo.

First of all, a college of 200 or so sovereign nations is about the size of a small village, which Maxwell admits might be able to exist without a common government. Second, a college of nations can deal with particular problems by creating councils or commissions without ceding their sovereignty to a government. They do this all the time.

Maxwell, however, seems to think that anyone in the role of a decision-maker is therefore a sovereign, which means that the people for whom he makes decisions have ceded their sovereignty.

This argument, however, is based on an equivocal use of the word "sovereign." There are three senses of sovereignty in his article:

1. the sovereign as a person who decides or who executes;
2. one who answers only to himself, i.e., the sovereign individual or the sovereign state; and
3. the people as sovereign, i.e., the idea that the common good of a people is the highest law of the land.

Maxwell's primary sense of sovereign is the first, a person who decides: "Who decides what rules? Who interprets?" Maxwell does not think that laws themselves can rule, because people must interpret and enforce them:

> Can we not all just agree to the rules? The affirmative answer to this question is known as *rule of law*, expressed pithily by Thomas Paine where he says that for absolutists the king is law, whereas for republicans the law is king. But the law can't issue executive orders, nor can it wield an M16 or deploy the national guard—you need a man to do that, a man with agency to defend the law and judgement to interpret it. The law is a tool for governance, but a tool can no more govern than a blueprint can build a bridge. The law can't rule, and because it *can't* rule, questions as to whether it *should* rule are unintelligible.

Maxwell's argument strikes me as problematic for two main reasons.

First, he might be setting up a strawman. Obviously, laws can't rule without human agents who interpret and apply them. But is this really what the rule of law means, i.e., a set of rules that anticipates all possible eventualities and that can be simply and deductively applied without need of human judgment, much less anyone to enforce them? There is definitely a strand of liberal thinking that would purge decision and prudence from government, thinking that these stand in the way of impartial justice and fairness. But this is a simple impossibility. Every regime today that embraces the rule of law also commissions hordes of functionaries to interpret and apply the law.

Every law-governed society doesn't require just one decider, but countless deciders. Decisions are needed in every branch of government: executives from cops on the beat to every rank of the military to the President or Prime Minister, judges from traffic courts to the supreme court, and legislators in every jurisdiction.

Second, the act of decision—even final decision—does not exhaust the concept of sovereignty. *Deciders are merely executives, merely functionaries, of the laws and the broader political system.* Contra Maxwell, laws are not the tools of deciders; rather, the deciders are tools of the system to interpret and enforce laws. Deciders are not sovereigns. They answer to the system that commissions them.

This is true even of "absolute" monarchs. Their offices are defined for them by the political system. The way they enter and leave office is defined by the political system, and their performance is graded by the ultimate standards of that political system, which is sovereignty in the third sense above, namely popular sovereignty: The people's common good is the highest law of the land.

This sense of sovereignty is primary because it serves as a norm that governs the other senses of sovereignty.

The reason that nation-states should be sovereign (the second sense) is that a sovereign homeland is the best way to secure the flourishing of a people. Sovereigns in the first sense (deciders) are empowered to make decisions for the common good of the people.

Popular sovereignty is primarily a *normative* concept. It is best articulated by Aristotle in his *Politics*.[2] Aristotle recognizes that in every regime, some govern, and others are governed. This is true in regimes ruled by one man, few men, or many men. He also notes that in every regime, a minority always governs the majority. This is even the case in popular regimes, since the voters are only a subset of the populace, which means that the majority of voters are almost inevitably a minority of the population as a whole. For Aristotle, a lawful government exists when the ruling minority pursues the people's common good, whereas an unlawful government pursues the ruling minority's private interests.

When one man rules lawfully, we have monarchy. When one man rules lawlessly, we have tyranny. When the few rule lawfully, we have aristocracy. When they rule unlawfully, we have oligarchy. When the many rule lawfully, we have what Aristotle calls "polity." When they rule unjustly, we have democracy.

Maxwell thinks it is an objection to popular sovereignty to observe that "[a]n organized minority will always rule over a disorganized majority." For Aristotle, however, it is no objection to the idea of popular sovereignty to note that power is inevitably concentrated in the hands of a minority. The question of whether sovereignty is popular or not is not determined by observing *who rules*, but rather *for whom* they rule: the common

---

[2] See Greg Johnson, "Introduction to Aristotle's *Politics*," in *From Plato to Postmodernism* (San Francisco: Counter-Currents, 2019).

good of society or the private good of the ruling faction.

Maxwell is also dismissive of the idea that the concept of sovereignty is primarily normative:

> Sovereignty is not a question of in whose interests the ruler should act. The father should act in the interests of his children; the children are not *ipso facto* sovereign over the family.

This is not precise. An Aristotelian would say that a good father rules the family in the interests of the whole family. Sovereignty is not located in persons at all, not the father or the children. The father is merely the executive of the family's common good. The children, by virtue of their helplessness, are merely recipients of parental care. Persons are mere functionaries within a justly ordered family, and their performance of their duties is graded by the common good of the family, and of the larger society of which they are parts.

Maxwell continues:

> Sovereignty is also often thought to be exhausted by the question of legitimacy—who *ought* to rule? But there is no ought without can. If it's not even possible in principle for the proletariat to rule, then the question of whether it should rule is moot. Who *can* rule? This question needs to be addressed first.

This, too, is imprecise. Sovereignty is not so much "exhausted" by the question of legitimacy, but legitimacy is definitely the most important question. Laws can't interpret or execute themselves. Laws therefore need functionaries to interpret and execute them. Whether these functionaries do a good job or a bad job, whether they are just or corrupt, depends on the inescapably *norma-*

tive question of *for whom* they are working: the common good of society or their own private interests? Power and the functionaries who exercise it are legitimate if they work for the common good, illegitimate if they do not.

Maxwell also fails to grasp that the idea of national sovereignty is primarily and essentially a normative concept, hence his claim that: "If your ability to decide is governed by someone else's veto, you are not sovereign."

Really? Your ability to decide *anything*? Even to do *wrong* things? Even to do injury to your neighbors? If I decide not to rob my neighbors, because that would inevitably provoke retaliation, and I must live with these people, is that decision not sovereign because it takes other people's interests and reactions into account? If I decide not to rob my neighbors because I would not want them to rob me, is that a violation of my sovereignty? If I decide that it is preferable to deal with my neighbors by means of persuasion rather than violence, is that a violation of my sovereignty? Is there such a thing as a *moral* "veto" of my will, a veto that I would impose upon myself because it is the right thing to do, a veto that my neighbors would impose upon me by retaliation because I richly deserve it?

Maxwell continues:

> If Canada wanted to invite the Chinese to place chemical weapons facilities on its southern border, America would swiftly shut that down. Much as it pains me to admit, Canada is not a sovereign nation. There are perhaps three or four sovereign nations today, and neither Canada nor Ukraine are among them.

This simply confuses sovereignty with military power, which means that weak nations are not sovereign because they can't do just anything they want to their neighbors. But on this account, no nations are really sovereign, because no nation is so powerful that it could not be destroyed by an alliance of other nations.

If we had a world in which strong nations could attack any weaker nations, and weak nations could band together to oppose strong nations, eventually, after a great deal of striving and bloodshed, peace would be achieved. At that point, it might occur to people that it would be simpler to just respect other nations' sovereignty from the start. This was why the concept of national sovereignty was invented in the first place: to bring an end to the orgy of bloodshed that convulsed Europe after the Reformation.

National sovereignty is a normative concept of international law. Under international law, all sovereign states are equal, and when one sovereign state attacks another, the attacker is *wrong* and the victim is *wronged*, even if the attacker is strong enough to get away with it. In such a situation, the proper response is not to do away with the concept of national sovereignty, but rather for other sovereign states to band together to force the offending state back into compliance with international law.

Although the bulk of Maxwell's article deals with sovereignty in the first two senses—the executive and national sovereignty—he frames his comments in terms of the issue of popular sovereignty, which he dismisses on the ground that the people cannot and do not rule. Order, he says, is imposed from the top down by small minorities. It does not bubble up spontaneously from the masses.

I have two objections to this line of reasoning.

First, framing the issue as "populism or vanguardism" misunderstands popular sovereignty's normative nature. Power is always exercised by minorities. Popular sovereignty is honored when minorities exercise power for the common good of society. Thus, every populist movement is also vanguardist.

Second, breezily dismissing popular sovereignty and populist politics based on Traditionalist and Neoreactionary dogmas is self-defeating. As I put it in the final paragraph of my essay, "In Defense of Populism":

> [Undemocratic] Liberalism triumphed not by rejecting popular sovereignty but by subverting it. This is one reason the elites are so hysterical about the rise of populism. It puts them on the spot. If they affirm popular sovereignty, then populism is the only logical outcome. If they deny popular sovereignty, good luck getting people to vote for that. Thus they'd rather avoid the argument entirely. But we can't let them. We need to press this advantage by demanding that they live up to the principle of popular sovereignty, which empowers the people they loathe. In a fair contest, illiberal democracy will beat undemocratic liberalism every time.[3]

Counter-Currents, November 4, 2022

---

[3] Greg Johnson, "In Defense of Populism," in *White Identity Politics* (San Francisco: Counter-Currents, 2020), p. 82.

Tucker Carlson on White Identity Politics

Tucker Carlson deserves a lot of thanks for being the most outspoken critic of the insanity of America's ruling family: the demented and abusive husband (the Democrats), the abused and clinging wife who enables him (the Republicans), their spoiled and insane daughter (the Left), and their increasingly aggressive Pitbull that they allow to bite people and befoul their neighborhood. Tucker speaks primarily for their abused and neglected son, the American people, who is now at risk from a whole range of self-destructive behaviors. I hope the kid makes it. He's lucky to have Uncle Tucker in his life.

I am particularly grateful that Mr. Carlson has spoken openly about the Great Replacement: the ongoing demographic decline of white nations due to Third World immigration and low white birthrates. The Great Replacement is a truly magical concept. If you object to the Great Replacement, it is an evil Right-wing conspiracy theory that merits censorship and imprisonment. If you celebrate it, however, you can be published by the *New York Times*.

But as useful as Mr. Carlson has been to advocates of white identity politics like me, he is *not* one of us, as he made clear in a recent interview with Adam Carolla (I want to thank Jim Goad for transcribing this):

> I will say this, if I could just make one prediction. So the United States is becoming nonwhite. Everyone's excited about it. Or if you're not excited about it, it doesn't matter. Whites are going to be in the minority. So what that means—soon—so what that means is, you're gonna get, at some point probably in my lifetime, people standing up and saying, "I represent

white people! I'm the candidate of the white voter!"[1]

This is how I read Mr. Carlson's remarks so far: The Great Replacement is happening. All the dominant voices are celebrating it. If you don't celebrate it, that doesn't matter. They are not giving us any choice in the matter. Whites are going to be a minority. But if you attack people as white, eventually they are going to defend themselves as white. Thus, white identity politics is inevitable.

This is entirely correct.

In a democracy, becoming a minority means that we will lose even the chance of asserting political control over our own destiny. Of course, our current democracy is a sham, because we were never allowed to vote on the Great Replacement to begin with. It was imposed upon us by hostile elites.

How do we stop the Great Replacement? It is happening due to a whole array of anti-white policies. Obviously, we need to oppose them with pro-white policies. We need to craft policies that will reverse white demographic decline and promote white interests. We need politicians and pundits who will champion such ideas. And we need to rally voters to support pro-white policies. Of course, this primarily means white voters, although I am sure some non-whites also oppose the Great Replacement, since it erodes their political power, culture, and living standards as well. In sum, we need white identity politics.

Mr. Carlson may think white identity politics is inevitable, but he wants none of it:

> And I just wanna say, on the record, that I'm gonna tell that person to fuck off. Because nobody speaks—I'm a, I'm an adult man, and nobody speaks for me 'cause he shares the same skin color as me. I just re-

---

[1] https://adamcarolla.com/tucker-carlson-4/

ject that entire idea. If I agree with you, I'll let you speak for me, and if I don't, I won't. But this idea that someone of a certain skin color, any skin color, or any ethnic background speaks automatically on behalf of all people who share that skin color or ethnic background is a Nazi idea, and I'm totally opposed to it. And I will be opposed to it when it happens to me. When some—this will happen—someone's gonna, "Oh, white people!" And I'll be like, "I don't even know you, dude. I don't even know you. I refuse to allow you to purport to speak for me 'cause we look the same, period."

Mr. Carlson is objecting to two issues here. He objects to the idea of someone who represents white ethnic interests, and he rejects the idea of white ethnic interests themselves. Mr. Carlson's objection to both ideas hinges on the concept of choice.

Mr. Carlson does not like the idea that people will emerge someday soon claiming to represent his interests as a white person. He's an adult, and he says he will choose who represents him based on whether he agrees with him or not.

I think that Mr. Carlson, like many conservatives, would like to go back to an era before identity politics, when voters chose who represented them based on ideology, not identity.

A lot of conservatives don't like identity politics because it bases political representation on something that we don't choose: our identities. This, of course, is a deeply *liberal* assumption, namely that *anything unchosen is illegitimate.*

But there are many things we don't choose. We don't choose to be born. We don't choose where we are born. We don't choose our parents. We don't choose our sex. We don't choose our mother tongue. And, of course, we don't choose our race.

We might prefer not to have any enemies. But sometimes, we are given no choice, because our enemies also have the power to choose us.

We would also prefer that our enemies do not attack us, but they might have their own plans.

Finally, we would prefer that our enemies not attack us where we are weak, but that's precisely where they will aim.

Right now, the Left attacks whites as whites, and they will continue to do so as long as white people refuse to fight back as whites. That flank is left undefended because of an absurd taboo against white identity politics (and *only* white identity politics).

Because whiteness is undefended, loonies are now attacking everything they score badly on—beauty, cleanliness, punctuality, literacy, numeracy, rationality, Body Mass Indexes, really any standards whatsoever—as white things.

The stakes, then, are extremely high. Civilization itself is in the balance. Moreover, Mr. Carlson recognizes that white people are being attacked as white people. But because he has internalized the silly taboo against defending white interests, he's not yet comfortable fighting back as a white person, which he makes clear elsewhere in the same interview:

> Well, I mean, the whole thing, everything about it is shocking to me, including the fact that people put up with it. The endless attacks on the whites, and I'm not defending whites—plenty of them, in fact, most of the people who annoy me are white, okay— but to attack any group as a group is by definition, like, a Nazi move.

But the old paradigm Mr. Carlson prefers is not coming

back. Why? Because there are only two ways to defeat anti-white identity politics. One way is to beat them with white identity politics, which means embracing identity politics. The other way is to persuade the anti-whites to give up identity politics altogether and go back to the old model, which they will never do.

Imagine American politics as a poker game. In this game, every racial, ethnic, and other identity group has a seat at the table and a stack of chips. Whites are the largest group, so we've got the biggest stack of chips. But the way the game is played is that every other group has a wild card, namely the "race card" or the "identity card," but white people don't.

You would never consent to playing poker by those rules, because no matter how many advantages you had at the start of the game, every hand you play is going to bring you closer and closer to losing it all. The only way not to lose that game is not to play it.

The way to stop playing that game is to give up the ridiculous taboo against white identity politics. White people simply need to say, "We're in an ethnic battle, and we're taking our own side. Not taking your own side in a fight is the mark of a liberal. We're not going to be swindled out of our birthright by playing by these rigged rules."

Republicans, however, believe that white identity politics is evil *per se*. *Only* white identity politics is evil, however, since Republicans are eager to pander to blacks, Hispanics, Asians—really, anybody but whites. At this point, the only thing conservatives have left is the idea that white identity politics is a "Nazi" thing—as if they would judge any other group's identity politics by the worst-case scenario. Interestingly enough, that's the same thing that anti-whites say to keep us from fighting back.

Since Republicans will not embrace white identity politics, they can only try to persuade other groups to abandon their own identity politics. But why would any sane group voluntarily drop a *winning* strategy? Why would they exchange a winning strategy for a losing one? Why would they follow the example of losers instead of holding them in contempt?

Beyond that, even if we could go back to the old paradigm of ideological rather than identity politics, it was hardly a winning strategy for the Right. Since the end of the Cold War, Republicans have done little more than weakly protest and then gracefully capitulate to every one of the Left's destructive demands.

Mr. Carlson's comments are a wonderful illustration of the power of moral ideas to shape politics. He represents the best of the conservative movement. He sees the Great Replacement. He understands that anti-white identity politics will make white identity politics inevitable. He might even see that mobilizing around whiteness is necessary to defeat the anti-white Left. Yet, he is held back by a classical liberal discomfort with unchosen political loyalties, which leads him to reject identity politics. (At least he is consistent in rejecting identity politics for everyone.) This is why philosophy is so important to our cause. Once these sorts of dogmas are destroyed, white identity politics will be unstoppable.

Counter-Currents, April 7, 2023

CHRISTOPHER RUFO ON WHITE IDENTITY POLITICS

Christopher Rufo is an outspoken conservative critic of Critical Race Theory (CRT) and the bizarre excesses of "sex ed" in today's schools. He is a fellow at the Manhattan Institute and the author of *America's Cultural Revolution: How the Radical Left Conquered Everything* (New York: Broadside Books, 2023).

To his credit, Rufo has actually influenced policy in a positive direction, including Donald Trump's 2020 executive order banning diversity training in the federal government and the 2022 Florida bill banning pedophile teachers from "grooming" students—at least until the fourth grade.

Rufo is married to a Thai woman, with whom he has fathered three mixed-race children. Thus it is unsurprising that he is no friend of white identity politics, as he makes clear in a recent *City Journal* article, "No to the Politics of 'Whiteness': The Case Against Right-Wing Racialism."[1]

Rufo correctly identifies Critical Race Theory as anti-white identity politics. But his preferred alternative to CRT is "colorblind" individualism, rather than pro-white identity politics:

> Unfortunately, some on the right would snatch defeat from the jaws of victory, preferring instead to adopt the basic framework of identity politics and simply reverse its polarity. Dismayingly, a senti-

---

[1] Christopher Rufo, "No to the Politics of 'Whiteness': The Case Against Right-Wing Racialism," *City Journal*, August 30, 2023.

ment is rising in some corners of conservative politics that the answer to left-wing identity politics is right-wing identity politics.

I am an advocate of white identity politics. Indeed, I have authored books like *The White Nationalist Manifesto*[2] and *White Identity Politics*,[3] so naturally I was interested in Rufo's critique.

Before Rufo criticizes white identity politics, he summarizes the argument for it:

> The main argument for this position is that colorblind equality is unattainable. Left-wing racialism has been embedded in our institutions, laws, and policies to such an extent that it cannot be rolled back using conventional means.

Rufo does not cite any sources, and I don't know of any advocates of white identity politics that hold precisely this view.

First, I wouldn't argue that colorblind equality is "unattainable," especially because of a contingent and alterable fact like Leftist institutional power. Instead, I believe that colorblind equality is *possible*. I just think it is *undesirable*, because it would lead to dystopian results.

Not all behavior is biologically determined, but a lot of it is. Beyond that, there are clear biological differences between the races. To simplify matters, let's just talk about blacks and whites. If blacks and whites were to live under a system of colorblind equality—and by "equality," Rufo means equality before the law, not equality of out-

---

[2] Greg Johnson, *The White Nationalist Manifesto* (San Francisco: Counter-Currents, 2018).

[3] Greg Johnson, *White Identity Politics* (San Francisco: Counter-Currents, 2020).

comes—there would be no affirmative action, and all efforts to go soft on black crime would be wiped away. Thus blacks would be much poorer than at present (because of genes for low IQs and high time preferences) and even more of them would be in jail (because of genes for low empathy and high impulsiveness).

Therefore, blacks would be even unhappier and more rebellious than they are now. Moreover, they would not be receptive to the claim that this is just colorblind meritocracy at work. Instead, they would see it as the oppressive imposition of *white* standards of behavior on a different race. And they would be right. What Rufo thinks is universal civilization is just white civilization, and although other races wish to share in the fruits of our civilization, they find submitting to its discipline to be oppressive and alienating.

What could Rufo do in the face of this? Call for more policing and more incarceration, and promise that his colorblind utopia is just over the horizon? Wouldn't it be simpler and more humane to simply give black Americans their own homeland and be done with it? After all, black Americans are a distinct people. Black and white Americans are far more different genetically and culturally than, say, the Norwegians and the Swedes, who have their own sovereign states. The alternative is for white Americans to forever resent blacks for retarding white civilization and blacks to forever seethe at whites for imposing it upon them in the first place.

Beyond that, if Rufo were to achieve a workable colorblind, multiracial society, it would presumably dismantle all barriers to interracial marriage. I find this alarming. Whites are a global minority with below replacement fertility in all our homelands. If nothing is done to change this, we will go extinct.[4] Promoting race-

---

[4] See Greg Johnson, "White Extinction," in *The White Na-*

mixing will simply hasten our doom. I regard white extinction with horror. I cannot countenance any policy that promotes it.

Rufo continues:

> All politics is friend-enemy politics, this faction argues, and given the demographic decline of European Americans, whites will eventually need to activate "white racial consciousness" to secure their basic interests. European Americans once had robust ethnic identities, but after generations of assimilation and intermarriage, those distinctions have lost their salience and consolidated into a homogenous, generalized "white identity." If there is to be a racial spoils system, then each group must get its share—including whites.

Again, Rufo cites no sources. But he's basically right, although I have two quibbles.

First, I don't think it is right to oppose "ethnicity" to "white identity." White Americans are not generic white people. We are a distinct ethnic group: Americans.[5] It used to go without saying that Americans are white people, hence the existence of hyphenated terms like African-American and Asian-American. White people are just American-Americans.

Second, if white Americans are to survive in a multiracial, multicultural society, we need to get uppity,[6] think collectively, and start taking our own side.[7] But I

---

tionalist Manifesto.

[5] Greg Johnson, "American Ethnic Identity," in *In Defense of Prejudice*.

[6] Greg Johnson, "Uppity White Folks and How to Reach Them" and "The Uppity White Folks Manifesto," in *White Identity Politics*.

[7] Michael Polignano, "Taking Our Own Side," in his *Taking*

advocate this kind of white identity politics only as an interim solution. I don't want white Americans to be locked in zero-sum racial struggles till the end of time, even if we come out on top. Thus I advocate racial divorce.[8]

Rufo acknowledges that anti-white racism is deeply embedded in America today. He also acknowledges that racial categories are "useful shorthand descriptors for many purposes." But this still does not justify "the racialist argument, which is wrong on moral, political, and pragmatic grounds."

I wish to focus on Rufo's moral argument, which is the substance of his piece. His political and pragmatic arguments strike me as mere throwaways.

> First, the right-wing racialists employ the same reductive demographic arguments as their left-wing counterparts, presenting American life as a zero-sum conflict between ethnic and racial groups, while ignoring the two other essential units of categorization: the individual and the universal. A more fruitful analysis would begin with a full accounting of these categories—individual, ethnicity, race, and humanity—and build a political theory capable of organizing them in the interest of human flourishing.

This isn't really an argument. First, both Left and Right are *factually correct* that America is locked in a zero-sum racial death match between white Americans and non-whites. Rufo does not challenge this fact. Indeed, he admits it. But he prefers to change the subject to "the indi-

---

Our Own Side (San Francisco: Counter-Currents, 2010).

[8] Greg Johnson, "Irreconcilable Differences: The Case for Racial Divorce," in *Truth, Justice, & a Nice White Country*.

vidual and the universal."

Rufo claims that "ethnicity" and "race" should have places in a "full accounting." But I notice that in the rest of his article, ethnicity and race drop out of the picture, because on his account, all humans have the same rights, which are borne by individuals. Thus Rufo would never countenance "group rights" to preserve distinct cultures and races that trump individual rights to destroy them.

Rufo continues:

> Fortunately, such a political theory already exists: the natural rights theory of the American Founders, who argued that each human being was endowed with "certain unalienable rights" that applied to all as a universal principle; at the same time, they accepted that, because human cultures are contingent, not all groups will have identical capacities, expressions, and outcomes.
>
> This approach remains the best available.

The American founders did not envision a multiracial society. They saw America as a white nation. Blacks and Indians may have been "in" America, but they were not "of" it.

But this does not contradict the idea that all men have rights to life, liberty, and the pursuit of happiness. Thomas Jefferson, who wrote the Declaration of Independence—which is not, by the way, a legal document of the United States—also wrote that blacks and whites, "equally free, cannot live in the same government."[9] Why? Because "Nature, habit, opinion has drawn indelible lines of distinction between them." To use Rufo's words, because blacks and whites don't have "identical

---

[9] Thomas Jefferson, *Autobiography* (1821) (New York: Simon & Schuster, 2012), p. 40.

capacities," they will not produce identical "expressions" and "outcomes." And as Jefferson observed, these differences are based not just in culture, but in nature. Habits and opinions can be changed, but nature cannot.

Like Jefferson, I believe that all men have rights. Like Jefferson, I also believe that human differences can be so stark that not all types of men can flourish in the same polity. I wish other races well, but they are simply a bad fit for American society.

White Nationalism is not "un-American."[10] It is as American as the 1790 Naturalization Act, in which the founders wisely limited candidates for naturalization to free white people of good character. It is as American as the Asian Exclusion movement of the nineteenth century that protected free white laborers from being immiserated by competition from Asian immigrants. It is as American as the Immigration Act of 1924, wisely designed by its architects to maintain a white supermajority.

Rufo continues:

> The essential political questions for both supporters and opponents of the racialist worldview are these: What is the proper locus of rights? How should people be judged as a matter of government policy? And what approach is consistent with American principles and most likely to ensure our success as a nation?

I have already indicated why I think white identity politics is most "consistent with American principles and most likely to ensure our success as a nation," although I identify "our nation" with that of the founders and their posterity, while Rufo identifies our nation with the post-

---

[10] Greg Johnson, "Is White Nationalism Un-American?," in Toward a New Nationalism.

1965 multicultural experiment.
Rufo then adds:

> The honest racialist would respond: the proper locus of rights is the group; people should be judged in a race-conscious manner; and the best approach is the one that rewards friends and punishes enemies.

I agree with this when it comes to determining the boundaries between us and them. But within those boundaries, individuals should be treated as individuals. Individual freedom is a good thing, but whenever it conflicts with the common good of society, including our posterity, it must give way. America's founders would not disagree with this. They did not think of the Constitution as a suicide pact.

Rufo's credo, by contrast is:

> the proper locus of rights is the individual; people should be judged in a colorblind manner; and the best approach honors particularity while discouraging the formation of racial factions, foregrounds equality of rights while accepting inequality of outcomes, and acknowledges group differences while appealing to our equal dignity as human beings and as citizens of a common polity.

I find this problematic for three reasons.

First, simply allowing individuals to exercise their rights can lead to terrible consequences: the extinction of species and the degradation of the natural world, the collapse of living standards due to global capitalism, the destruction of communities due to multiculturalism and mass migration, and even the extinction of the white race, none of which classical liberals can object to "as long as it is voluntary."

Second, if one truly "honors particularity" and "acknowledges group differences," one would make provisions for groups to preserve their distinctness in the face of globalization, even if this limits individual rights to migrate, marry, and buy and sell as one pleases. Rufo's outlook dooms particularity and group differences in the long-run, despite paying them lip service.

Third, Rufo's colorblind individualism, far from "discouraging the formation of racial factions," actually *promotes* their flourishing to the detriment of the white majority. European individualism is a highly advantageous ethos. It has unleased enormous creativity in culture, science, technology, and commerce, creating immense wealth. It has also created peaceful, orderly, and humane societies. Unfortunately, the very success of European individualist societies makes them attractive to collectivist groups which have learned to hack and subvert them.

How do you cheat an individualist? You pretend to be an individualist while working as a member of a collective. You demand that individualists treat you as an individual in every transaction, but you do not reciprocate. Instead, whenever possible, you give preferences to members of your own tribe, and they give preferences to you.

Over time, as such unfair transactions multiply, collectivist cheats will amass wealth and power at the expense of individualist suckers. But the individualists will never catch on, *because they think that blindness to groups is a virtue.* By preaching the virtue of blindness to groups, Rufo is not resisting but promoting the destruction of white individualist societies.

This puts Rufo's accusation that white identity politics threatens to "snatch defeat from the jaws of victory" in an ironic light. The "victory" Rufo is speaking about is the feeble pushback against CRT by mainstream Rightists like himself. But CRT is merely one tool of non-white identity politics. Opposing CRT removes one weapon from the anti-white arsenal, but it does not strike against non-white identity politics as such.

Moreover, by pushing back against CRT in the name of colorblind individualism, Rufo is defending a losing strategy that, in the short to medium term, will allow collectivist cheats to continue hollowing out and wrecking white societies, thus promoting the destruction of everything that conservatives purport to conserve. Then, in the long run, it will lead to the extinction of the white race.

The only way to prevent individualist societies from being subverted is to recognize that individualism is not universal. It is very much a white thing, as Kevin MacDonald argues in *Individualism and the Western Liberal Tradition*.[11] And the only way to secure individualism against tribal cheats is to exclude such groups. But that sounds like collectivism and statism. Indeed it is. But individualist societies can only flourish in a bubble of collectivism and statism.

Rufo then sums up his moral argument:

> This approach is, in my view, consistent with the method (natural rights) and the ultimate *telos* (human happiness) that the Founders envisioned and that the Constitution and American law have gradually secured. The ultimate criterion of public judgement can either be race, leading toward a "prison yard society," or merit, leading toward an "aristocracy of virtue and talents." Choose one.

There are three problems here.

---

[11] Kevin MacDonald, *Individualism & the Western Liberal Tradition: Evolutionary Origins, History, & Prospects for the Future* (Kindle Direct Publishing, 2019).

First, America's founders never envisioned a universal, multiracial society. Nor do the ideas of natural rights or human flourishing lead to such a society. Again, all men may have rights, but that does not make just anyone a good fit for a white society, which is what the founders envisioned for themselves and their posterity.

Second, Rufo is implicitly buying into a Leftist narrative about America, namely that the founders promised universal equality to all people and that America must therefore be measured by that standard, in which case we still have "a lot of work to do." This is simply false.

Third, he ends with a blatant false alternative: racial prison yard or individualist aristocracy.

The prison yard analogy doesn't mean what Rufo thinks it means. America's prisons used to be much more peaceful because they were racially segregated. They became much more violent when they were integrated. The same is true of American society as a whole. Multiculturalism is an inherently violent ideology, which is why white identity politics wants to roll it back.

Moreover, I am all for talent and virtues, but I don't want to be ruled by talented and virtuous aliens, especially collectivist cheats who have risen to the top of American society by exploiting our virtues and turning them into disadvantages. Governments have terrifying power. It is too dangerous to put that power in the hands of people who feel no kinship with us, many of whom are also nursing ancient historical grudges against whites. Moreover, the white race has never had a shortage of talented and virtuous leaders who are also our own kin.

Rufo's final paragraph begins with a very cheap shot. He accuses racialists of the Right of being driven by "a sense of inferiority." And here I thought we were terrible snobs.

The only way for conservatives to head off white identity politics is to convince non-whites to abandon their identity politics and adopt colorblind individualism. Rufo thinks he's making progress in that area. All he needs to do is convince non-whites to drop a winning strategy for one that will increase the immiseration and incarceration of blacks and Hispanics, all because the losers demand that they "play fair." Yes, conservatives are that desperate and delusional. Obviously, it will never work. That's why the future belongs to white identity politics.

Counter-Currents, September 5, 2023

In Your Heart, You Know Ye's Right

I don't really have a dog in the fight between Kanye West and America's Jewish power structure, so I am just sitting back and enjoying the show. But I am pretty much certain that, no matter what the outcome for Mr. West, whites in America and around the world will benefit, and for that I am grateful. Thank you, Kanye, for your courage and sacrifice.

When I was a paleoconservative back in the 1990s, I began noticing that Jews played a disproportionate role in promoting destructive ideologies and social trends: Marxism, feminism, globalization, open borders, sexual liberation, political correctness, racial egalitarianism, and the absurd cult of the negro.

Beyond that, Jews were overrepresented among the forces opposed to solving these problems. Once the pattern became clear, scarcely a day has gone by without further confirmation.

This is not to say there are no good Jews. I know for a fact that that there are. There just aren't enough of them to change the disastrous course their community has put us on.

I am a firm believer in free speech. America has serious problems, but none of them are so bad that we can't solve them. But we can't solve them unless we can talk about them. Unfortunately, to protect their power, Jews have created a web of taboos and inhibitions—and beyond that, a climate of fear and intimidation—to make it impossible to even talk about the situation. If you want to corrupt even the noblest people, simply make them above criticism, then wait. If you want to destroy a society, just make its elites immune from criticism, and they'll do the rest.

Every serious person in America today knows that Jews are the most powerful and privileged group in society, but if you openly acknowledge that fact, they will destroy you. Jews are one of the most densely networked and collectivist groups in America today, but you aren't allowed to notice that fact. They can act as a team, but we have to pretend that they are just individuals. As Dave Chappelle put it, "If they're black, then it's a gang. If they're Italian, it's a mob. But if they're Jewish, it's a coincidence, and you should *never* speak about it."[1]

We also must pretend that we have no idea where any of this is going. I'll tell you where it's going. Since a team strategy beats an individualist strategy every time, the only place this is going is a tighter and tighter Jewish stranglehold, until America finally expires from decadence and diversity. But it all ends when white people start noticing and taking our own side.

We can't fix America without discussing the so-called Jewish Question.

If every important person in America today knows about Jewish power, why don't they just speak out about it? It is complicated. But the main reason is lack of solidarity. They all know that the game would be up if enough of them would speak out at the same time. But somebody must go first. And nobody wants to be first, because these people have more rivals than friends, and they know that their rivals would scramble to denounce them for speaking the truth. Why overthrow an unjust power structure, when you can simply suck up a notch or two by denouncing braver, more principled men? Thus a prominent American would have to be nuts to speak out about the Jews.

---

[1] Dave Chappelle, *Saturday Night Live* opening monologue, November 12, 2022.

Enter Kanye West.

Kanye West is 100% a product of America's Jewish power structure. Jews have promoted black music for more than 100 years and virtually created the rap industry. Jews have also created rampant negro worship throughout our culture, which has trained millions of intelligent whites to idolize blacks as entertainers, athletes, celebrities, and even intellectuals. Countless influential Americans have courted Kanye West, including Donald Trump and Barack Obama. They eagerly had their pictures taken with him, sharing them on social media to signal their virtue. They have patiently listened to his often incoherent talk, for fear of offending against the dominant taboos. Countless black criminals walk the streets today because West persuaded Donald Trump to implement sentencing reforms.

Kanye West flourished in this environment. He has sold more than 160 million records. He has received 22 Grammy Awards, which isn't bad for a guy who started in 2004. His name has been associated with such fashion brands as Louis Vuitton, Gap, Nike, Balenciaga, and Adidas. In 2005 and 2015 *Time* magazine named him one of the 100 Most Influential People in the world. In 2020, he ran for President of the United States. He has made 100s of millions of dollars, and recent deals pushed him into billionaire territory. Surely a Nobel prize or two was in the cards.

Kanye West is a Jewish Golem. But, like many of their Golems, he has now turned on them.

Kanye West is reportedly bipolar. If this is true, however, it does not invalidate what he is saying. Again, in America today, a billionaire who knows how the system works would have to be slightly crazy to speak the truth. And Kanye West has spoken openly about Jewish power.

Kanye West is not the spokesman I would choose, but his audience is bigger than those of my preferred spokesmen by orders of magnitude, and beggars can't be choosers. The people in our ranks who are complaining about this opportunity frequently come off like spoiled toddlers who won't eat their vegetables. Some gratitude would be in order.

There's nothing shameful about Kanye West challenging Jewish power. The shame is on his "betters" who are too calculating and cowardly to do the same.

Yes, West has said some dumb things, like blacks are the real Jews. Yes, he could have been more articulate. But, by and large, he has spoken the truth: Jews have disproportionate power in America, which they use to push the country to the Left, and they will punish anyone who speaks about it.

The results have been swift and instructive.

- After the predictable outcry from the Anti-Defamation League, West was dropped as a spokesman for Adidas, Balenciaga, Gap, and *Vogue*, causing his fortune to dip below one billion dollars.
- Footlocker and TJ Maxx removed his merchandise from their stores.
- West has been dropped by his largest bank, J.P. Morgan Chase.
- Jews are openly talking about the "taboo" status of "anti-Semitism," and establishment figures are falling over one another to denounce West.
- The controversy widened when Dave Chappelle essentially defended West in a brilliant *Saturday Night Live* monologue.
- Some, however, did not understand that Jews have higher status than blacks. Thus they were not quick enough to denounce West. This includes former President Donald Trump, who

invited West to dinner at Mar-a-Lago. West brought "anti-Semite" and "Holocaust denier" Nick Fuentes to dinner, and when the news that Trump dined with West and Fuentes got out, the whole planet began watching. Kanye West and Nick Fuentes could very well have brought down Donald Trump.

❖ West, Fuentes, and Milo Yiannopoulos went on Tim Pool's show, spoke rather eloquently about the Jewish Question, and then West walked out after Pool kept insisting that Jewish power is a coincidence that we should never speak about.

❖ West and Fuentes went on Alex Jones' show, whereupon a gimp-masked West not only refused to back down from his views on Jews but said that he loved Adolf Hitler, loved Nazis, and denied that six million Jews were killed in the Holocaust. (I honestly wish he had not done this. It gets the wrong people excited. It also smacks of retreat: about the only way out of this now is for West to paint himself as a slightly crazed religious crank who is to be pitied, not taken seriously.)

❖ Elon Musk suspended West's Twitter account. So much for his commitment to free speech.

❖ A wide swath of faux-edgy Right-wing e-celebs like Bronze Age Pervert have revealed that they are quite happy to hold down the Rightmost edge of the Jewish-dominated mainstream.

❖ There has been much comic seething from washed up Alt-Right e-celebs.

❖ Nick Fuentes and Milo Yiannopoulos, however, have openly stood up against Jewish power. Good for them.

I don't know what the future holds for Kanye West, but I fear for his freedom and ultimately for his life. An example must be made of him, to discourage other wealthy and influential people from speaking about Jewish power. But the best his enemies can do now is silence him and intimidate others, and they will still come off as villains. They can't change the fact that millions of people have noticed for the first time how Jewish power works. Now that they see the basic pattern, not a day will go by without further confirmation. And if Kanye West is martyred for challenging the Jewish power structure, well, we've seen that one before too.

Counter-Currents, December 2, 2022

How I Got Banned from the New "Free Speech" Twitter

I cheered when Elon Musk bought Twitter, promising to turn it into a free speech platform. I admit that I've never been crazy about Twitter. But it is one of the principal platforms hosting the liberal hive mind and its ever-shifting consensus, so anything that ventilates that echo-chamber is a good thing.

I had two Twitter accounts. The first, NewRightAmerica, was for Counter-Currents. The second, GregJohnsonPhD, was my personal account. I never invested much in either account. Neither account had many followers. The Counter-Currents account was banned a few years ago. (I found out about the ban on Gab.) My personal account was banned in December 2022 for "hate." The Tweet that got it taken down was a video excerpt from my essay "In Your Heart, You Know Ye's Right":

> Every serious person in America today knows that Jews are the most powerful and privileged group in society, but if you openly acknowledge that fact, they will destroy you. Jews are one of the most densely networked and collectivist groups in America today, but you aren't allowed to notice that fact. They can act as a team, but we have to pretend that they are just individuals. As Dave Chappelle put it, "If they're Black, it's a gang. If they're Italian, it's a mob. If they're Jewish, it's a coincidence, and you should never speak about it."
>
> We also must pretend that we have no idea where any of this is going. I'll tell you where it's going. Since a team strategy beats an individualist strategy every time, the only place this is going is a

tighter and tighter Jewish stranglehold, until America finally expires from decadence and diversity. But it all ends when white people start noticing and taking our own side.

We can't fix America without discussing the so-called Jewish Question.

If every important person in America today knows about Jewish power, why don't they just speak out about it? It is complicated. But the main reason is lack of solidarity. They all know that the game would be up if enough of them would speak out at the same time. But somebody must go first. And nobody wants to be first, because these people have more rivals than friends, and they know that their rivals would scramble to denounce them for speaking the truth. Why overthrow an unjust power structure, when you can simply suck up a notch or two by denouncing braver, more principled men? Thus a prominent American would have to be nuts to speak out about the Jews.

Enter Kanye West.

This is protected political speech under the American First Amendment, which should be the sole "term of service" at the new Twitter. However, Twitter still regulates "hate speech," in violation of the First Amendment.

The organized Jewish community is the principal driving force against the US First Amendment. Pointing that out, of course, is also defined as "hate speech." It is also "hate speech" to note that the Anti-Defamation League is the principal force protesting Musk's promise to allow free speech on Twitter.

There's no question that Musk has improved Twitter immensely. His exposure of the collaboration between Twitter, the Democratic Party, Left NGOs, and the American deep state to fix the 2020 election is particularly explosive. It is also quite satisfying to see antifa doxing accounts banned, and I hope there will be full transparency about the collusion between the old Twitter and such domestic terrorist groups as antifa and Black Lives Matter.

My fear, however, is that when the dust settles at Twitter, the Right-wing voices on the platform will be entirely "kosher," which means that Jews will still be policing the outer boundaries of acceptable speech. This would be a disaster, because there's no way to fix America without a free and open conversation about the Jewish question. Until Twitter is no longer ADL-occupied territory, Counter-Currents and other corners of the Internet will have to keep the First Amendment alive.

But don't give up on Elon Musk. He's obviously making it up as he goes along. He's obviously more of a people-pleaser than a man of principle. But if he wants to save free speech, he eventually must give the ADL a hard "no."

Musk may well have been naïve about who he is up against when he first got involved in Twitter. He may not have understood who he was fighting when he declared war on "the woke mind virus."

Of course, Jonathan Greenblatt of the ADL immediately knew where this was leading. But Elon Musk is a rocket scientist. Eventually, who he is up against is going to sink in.

Counter-Currents, December 16, 2022

Dave Chappelle:
Non-White Ally of the Year

Each year, Jared Taylor's *American Renaissance* names a "White Renegade of the Year," a tradition begun by Wilmot Robertson's *Instauration*. The white renegade of the year is someone who could have used his position to help whites but instead chose to do the opposite. In the same spirit, *Counter-Currents* is inaugurating a "Non-White Ally of the Year" series, to recognize non-whites who have used their position to help whites.

In 2022, Kanye West—whose popularity and reach came as quite a shock to me—received enormous coverage for wearing a White Lives Matter t-shirt. But that was soon eclipsed by the controversy he created by openly discussing Jewish power and privilege. I was grateful to Kanye for speaking the truth about the regime's ultimate taboos, at great personal cost to himself.

Others in the movement had reactions to Kanye ranging from cool to hostile.

- ❖ Some people view the movement as primarily a safe space to express racial hatred. I am all for free speech, but politics is more than primal scream therapy. It requires changing minds and building alliances, which require more disciplined discourse.
- ❖ Some people claim that praising non-whites for the good things they do is equivalent to adopting multiracialism. I doubt anyone honestly believes this, but it floats around nonetheless. No, I don't want a multiracial society. But I recognize that some non-whites might also have the same ethnonationalist and sepa-

ratist goals. Beyond that, some non-whites might promote ideas conducive to white ethnonationalism even if it is not what they themselves want. It is possible for people who are not White Nationalists, or even white, to contribute to our cause. This is why we have concepts like "allies" and "fellow travelers": to designate people who are *not us*, yet who are useful for attaining our political goals.

❖ Others decried Kanye West for being clownish and inarticulate. But that's hardly the point. The reason Kanye made such a splash is that he's famous and influential. His audience is far larger than Kevin MacDonald's, even though MacDonald is far more dignified and articulate. If Kanye's antics increase awareness of the Jewish Question, that's a good thing, regardless of his communication skills.

❖ Beyond that, Kanye West's statements are far less instructive than the establishment's reaction. The organized Jewish community, spearheaded by the ADL, declared war on Kanye, and within days he lost more than a billion dollars. That's astonishing. Indeed, the inarticulateness and clownishness of Kanye's statements make it all the more astonishing. Jews could have simply ignored or patronized Kanye. "Kanye, bro, are you okay?" But instead, they went "DEATH CON three" on him and knocked him out of the billionaire club. That's power. Reckless, vindictive, unaccountable power. We'd be better off without it.

Despite all this, Kanye West is not *Counter-Currents'* "Non-White Ally of the Year." Instead, that honor goes to comedian Dave Chappelle for his superb *Saturday Night*

Live monologue of November 12, 2022. I was first introduced to Chappelle more than a decade ago by my friend Mike Van Houten, who correctly saw Chappelle as an ally because he relentlessly mocked political correctness, especially about race.

Chappelle's monologue surpasses Kanye West's very real contributions for two reasons:

- ❖ Chappelle commented on Kanye's remarks and the Jewish reaction in an eloquent and genuinely funny manner.
- ❖ As Andrew Hamilton discusses in a classic article, "Join the Dance!,"[1] the difference between a lone nut and the leader of a movement is the first person to follow. Now, in the case of Kanye, it doesn't matter if Nick Fuentes and Milo Yiannopoulos jumped on board, because they are marginal. It is far more important for another mainstream figure to stand up for Kanye, specifically to amplify his message, criticize the reaction, and affirm the importance of free speech. Chappelle did these things, potentially at great cost to himself.

As a bonus, Chappelle also commented on Trump and Trump Derangement Syndrome, the Ukraine War, and white discontent in the wake of the 2022 midterm election. You can watch Chappelle's monologue online. I have also transcribed it, with comments.

Thank you. Thank you very much for being here. Before I start tonight, I just wanted to read a brief

---

[1] Andrew Hamilton, "Join the Dance!," *Counter-Currents*, September 24, 2010.

statement that I prepared: "I denounce anti-Semitism in all its forms, and I stand with my friends in the Jewish community." And that, Kanye, is how you buy yourself some time.

The rote manner in which Chappelle reels off the statement smacks of duress, implying from the start that Kanye and others in the same position are victims of coercion.

I gotta tell you guys, I probably been doing this for 35 years now. And early in my career, I learned that there are two words in the English language that you should never say together in sequence, and those words are "the" and "Jews." Never heard someone do good after they said that.

This makes one wonder: What bad things happen to people who speak about "the Jews"? *Who* makes those things happen? To be specific, Chappelle has been in *show business* for 35 years. What's the connection between "the Jews" and show business?

Kanye's gotten into some scrapes before. Normally when he was in trouble, I pull up immediately. This time I was like, "You know what, let me see what's gonna happen first."

Why would Chappelle adopt a wait and see attitude at this particular juncture? Obviously, the suggestion is that there is something especially dangerous in talking about "the Jews."

Can't remember how it started. Vaguely I remember it started with a tweet, strange tweet. It was like uh, "I'm feeling a little sleepy. I gonna get me some rest. But when I wake up, I'm gonna go DEATH CON three on the Jews," and then he just went to bed. I was up all night worried. What is he gonna do to the Jews?

I grew up around Jewish people. I have a lot of Jewish friends. So I'm not freaked out by your culture. I know a little bit about it just from hanging around. "Yo, let's go out after school tomorrow." But, like, "We can't go out. It's 'Shanana' tomorrow." I'm like, "What? What is 'Shanana'?" Like, I had so many questions. "Why do some of your people dress like Run DMC?"

When Kanye woke up from that nap, he went right to work.

A year ago, I'd seen him on a podcast called *Drink Champs*. Great show. And it was it was an amazing appearance. Noriega and them were there, the rappers that I love. And they all had their gold chains and stuff on, and Kanye said, "Only millionaires wear chains." They said, "What?" He said, "I'm a *billionaire*. Billionaires don't wear their money on their body." I tucked my chain, and I said, "Oh, snap."

It was a good appearance. It was fun and funny.

But when he woke up, he went on *Drink Champs* again. This time he was on one. He was mad about something. He said, "I can say *anti-Semitic* things. And Adidas can't drop me! Now what?"

Adidas dropped that nigger immediately. Ironically, Adidas was founded by Nazis, and *they* were offended. I guess the student has surpassed the teacher.

It's a big deal. He had broken the show business rules. This is a rule. You know, the rules of perception: If they're black, then it's a gang. If they're Italian, it's a mob. But if they're Jewish, it's a coincidence, and you should *never* speak about it.

I will be quoting those last three sentences for the rest of my life. They memorably sum up "the rules of perception" that extend far beyond show business. Of course, those rules work to the benefit of the people who created them: Jews. According to these rules, it is permissible to notice when lesser peoples work together in groups for their own interests. But when Jews work together as a group for their own interests, we must take no notice. We must pretend that it is just a coincidence. They're just individuals. There's nothing to see here. Hey, look over there . . .

Kanye got in so much trouble, Kyrie got in trouble. Kyrie Irving posted a link to a movie that he had seen on Amazon. No caption on the post or nothing like that. But apparently this movie had some, I don't know, "anti-Semitic tropes" or something. It was some weird title like *From Hebrew to Negro* or something. And the NBA told him he should apologize, and he was slow to apologize, and then the list of demands to get back in their good graces got longer and longer—and this is where, you know, I draw the line. I know the Jewish people have been through terrible things all over the world, but you can't blame that on black Americans; you just can't. You know what I mean? [audience member whoops] Thanks to the one person that said "whoo." A fair punishment would be he should just post a link to *Schindler's List*, and y'all write your own captions. Because Kyrie Irving's black ass was nowhere near the Holocaust. In fact, he's not even certain it existed.

This is brilliant, too. Chappelle puts his sympathy for victims of anti-Semitism right on the table, then he says that it is not an eternal excuse for bullying people who had nothing to do with it. But that's precisely the role that anti-Semitism, especially the Holocaust, plays in Jewish power today. It is a weapon of ethnic aggression, wielded under the cloak of ethnic victimhood.

Of course, Chappelle defends black Americans in particular, but the list of victims of Jewish bullying is far longer than that. Really, it encompasses the whole planet.

Jews were apoplectic, but why should they be? Aren't we all equal? Don't we live in a multicultural society, under conditions of equality? Shouldn't there be rules? Shouldn't we feel comfortable taking our own side when other groups bully us? Of course, there is no equality between Jews and other groups, as we have seen with the "rules of perception" outlined above.

Chappelle's last line is a real punch in the gut, because it makes clear that he's defending "Kyrie Irving's black ass" *even if* he had denied the Holocaust. Is nothing sacred? No. Not to Chappelle. Not to a genuinely free society.

> I saw one news pundit screaming about Kanye. She said, "Mental health is no excuse for that type of language." Yes, it is bitch. You can kill somebody if you're mentally ill. Listen, okay. I don't think Kanye is crazy, at all. I think he's possibly . . . not well.
>
> I've been to Hollywood. I don't want ya'll to get mad at me. I'm just telling you. I've been to Hollywood. This is just what I saw. It's *a lot* of Jews. Like a lot. But that doesn't mean anything. You know what I mean? There's a lot of black people in Ferguson, Missouri. Doesn't mean we run the place.

This too is very effective. Chappelle states the truth about what he has seen in Hollywood: a lot of Jews. Once that is out there, you really can't take it back. But then he does the Tim Fool thing, the Alex Jones thing: He declares it doesn't mean anything. But of course it means something. It isn't just a coincidence, after all. The analogy between Ferguson and Hollywood is transparently lame. We've already seen that the rules of show business privilege Jews over blacks. Who makes the rules of show business? Obviously, the people who run the place.

> I can see if you had some kind of issue, you know what I mean? You might go out to Hollywood, and your mind might start connecting some kind of lines, and you could maybe adopt the *delusion* that the Jews run show business. It's not a *crazy* thing to think. But it's a crazy thing to say out loud, in a climate like this.

Again, this is brilliant. Chappelle is saying that if a sane person observes the movie business and connects the dots, he might conclude that Jews run the place. It isn't crazy to think that. Why, then, is it crazy to say it? Because the people who run the place, namely Jews, might take things away from you.

> Now the midterms are over, in this crazy climate, and I gotta tell you, I feel like this midterm, like all of humanity depends on it. And it's an ominous sign. The most ominous sign of the midterms I believe would be Herschel Walker, who I don't want to speak badly of because he's black. But I have to admit. He's, umm . . . he's observably stupid. And even when he's not talking, his mouth be open a little bit. He's the kind of guy who looks like he thinks before he makes a move on tic tac toe.

If you are the kind of person who needs permission from a black celebrity to call black people stupid, Dave Chappelle has now written you a pass.

Watching the news now, they're declaring the end of the Trump era. Now, okay, I can see how in New York, you might believe that this is the end of his era. I'm just being honest with you. I live in Ohio, amongst the poor whites. A lot of you don't understand *why* Trump was so popular, but I get it because I hear it every day. He's very loved. And the reason he's loved is because people in Ohio have never seen somebody like him. He's what I call an honest liar. I'm not joking right now. He's an honest liar.

That first debate. That first debate. I've never seen anything like it. I've never seen a white male billionaire *screaming* at the top of his lungs: "This whole system is rigged," he said. And across the stage was a white woman, Hillary Clinton, and Barack Obama sitting over there looking at him like, "No, it's not." I said, "Now, wait a minute, bro, it's what he said." And the moderator said, "Well, Mr. Trump, if in fact the system is rigged, as you suggest, what would be your evidence?" Remember what he said, bro? He said, "I know the system is rigged, because I use it." I said "God*damn!*"

And then he pulled out an Illuminati membership card, chopped a line of cocaine up, and did it right at the podium.

No one had ever heard someone say something that true.

And then Hillary Clinton tried to punch him in the taxes. She said, "This man doesn't pay his taxes." He shot right back, "That makes me smart."

And then he said, "If you want me to pay my

taxes, then change the tax code. But I know you won't, because your friends and your donors enjoy the same tax breaks that I do." And with that, my friends, a star was born.

No one had ever seen a thing like that. No one had ever seen somebody come from inside of that house outside and tell all the commoners, "We're doing everything that you think we are doing inside of that house." And he just went right back in the house and started playing the game again.

This is brave, true, and genuinely hilarious.

> The Democrats were sore losers. I'm a Democrat. I'm telling you as soon as he won, they started saying all that "He's colluding with Russia; he's colluding with Russia." It was very embarrassing as a Democrat. But as time went on, we all came to learn, he was probably colluding with Russia. I even look at his wife different now. His wife is beautiful, no question about it, but she looks like the kinda chick that James Bond would smash but not trust.
>
> Why he got all them documents at his house? What is this? This guy is famous for not reading his press briefings. Now all of a sudden you get 10,000 documents in his house, gonna catch up on his reading list.
>
> I've been fired from jobs many times in my life, and I will be very honest with you. Sometimes when I was fired, I stole things from the office. Staplers, computer mouses, all kinds of stuff. You know what I never stole from work? *Work!*

It is nice to have a Democrat on record saying that the Russia collusion accusation was simply Democrats being sore losers. But the rest of this bit is incredibly lame. Maybe Chappelle actually believes it. Or maybe he's just giving the audience a rest from having their dogmas challenged.

> War in Ukraine brought it all into focus, and lucky for everybody in the Western world the Ukrainians are way better fighters than we thought they'd be. These guys, God bless'em, they're doin' good. They killed 10,000 Russians the first week of the war. Even the Vietnamese were like, "Goddamn, them some good numbers."
> This is before they had weapons. Before we started sending weapons. They was killing Russians with things you can find around the house. That whole country, Ukraine, is littered with traps like *Home Alone*. They was stepping on rakes. How is Russia losing to the Ukraine? That would be like America losing a war to Colorado.

This is genuinely funny, but it is calculated to appeal to the New York audience. Again, I think Chappelle might just be letting them relax a bit. He's lulling them into a sense of security before delivering a knockout blow.

> Now the midterms are over, and everybody's awake. These new whites, man, they're like newborn babies. Just woke up. Everything white people mad about, we've been on that. "Man, I can't feed my family." Black people like, "We been on that." "We can't trust the government." "We been on that!" "Man, we should dismantle the FBI!" Word to Martin Luther King, Bro. "We been on that!"

Dave Chappelle just offered social validation to whites

awakening to the idea that that the system is no longer theirs. I guess we can forget about white privilege. This is subversive, but it is treated as a bit of a throwaway before the final assault, where he returns to Kanye:

> Nobody listens to me when I tell these jokes. You know what I mean? My first Netflix special, what did I say? I said I don't want a sneaker deal, because the minute I say something that makes those people mad, they're gonna take my sneakers away, and the whole crowd's like, "Ha ha ha ha ha." Now you see Kanye walking around LA barefoot with his chain out. A billion and a half dollars in a day. A billion and a half dollars in a day. I said, "Put your chain on, nigger. Welcome back!"

Corporate sponsors are enemies of free speech. But, of course, none of this would have happened to Kanye if he had not spoken about Jewish power. As if to prove Kanye's point, Jews flexed their power and knocked him out of the billionaire club. The line "Put your chain on, nigger" is pregnant, because before black millionaires wore chains, black slaves wore them. Jews have reduced Kanye West to a barefoot "nigger" in chains because he spoke up about Jewish power. This is very provocative rhetoric, especially for blacks in the audience.

> It shouldn't be this scary to talk—about anything. This is making my job incredibly difficult, and to be honest with you, I'm getting sick of talking to a crowd like this. I love you to death, and I thank you for your support. And I hope they don't take anything away from me . . . *whoever they are.*

Dave Chappelle is a strong defender of free speech. Chappelle is a comedian, and comedy is the first casualty of wokeness. But Chappelle ends by pointing out that there are *people* behind political correctness. Somebody wrote the rules of wokeness. Somebody enforces the rules of wokeness. Somebody benefits from the rules of wokeness. And Kanye West's fate shows that calling them out is dangerous business, *whoever they are.*

Because Dave Chappelle has spotlighted the issue of Jewish power and privilege with intelligence, wit, and courage, he is *Counter-Currents*' Non-White Ally of the Year for 2022.

Counter-Currents, January 2, 2023

Why White Nationalists Didn't Want a Red Wave

It is Friday, November 11th, 2022, and if America is the greatest nation in the world, why do we still not know the final results of Tuesday's midterm elections?

Two things, however, are clear.

First, we knew going into this election that no matter who wins, the losers will regard the outcome as illegitimate, because each half of the electorate regards the other half as too dangerous to hold power. This means that an American people no longer exists. Instead, there are two hostile nations—or, rather, many hostile nations arrayed against each other in two blocs—sharing the same territory and government and creeping toward the realization that separation or bloody conflict are their only long-term options.

Second, we now know there was no "red wave." Instead, both parties will remain about equally balanced, which means more gridlock.

This is too bad for Republicans. But for White Nationalists, this is the best outcome, for three reasons.

First, the Republicans were counting on pure backlash politics to sweep them into power. They were counting on the public voting *against* the dastardly Democrats, so they were not interested in giving the people anything or anyone worth voting *for*. That would require the courage to court controversy. It would also require making promises that they would then have to break. Why do any of that when a backlash can put you in power with a blank check to do whatever your donors want? Hence, the Republicans fielded a horde of bland centrists, including large numbers of non-white and female diversity candidates. Wouldn't you love to have listened in to the Republican conclaves that decided to run the babbling, moronic gridiron groid Herschel Walker? In short, the red wave was standard Stupid Party shenanigans. It should not have been rewarded by the voters, and it wasn't.

Second, what White Nationalists want in a candidate is someone who caters to our interests: principally, upholding white standards in all areas of politics and culture and working to halt and then reverse white demographic decline. Barring that, we want candidates who will inject our issues into political debates, as Trump did by questioning the value of immigration and economic globalization, and who will enact legislation that will help slow the Great Replacement, particularly immigration controls.

In this election, I was rooting for a few candidates who were more nationalist and populist than the Republican mainstream: Ron DeSantis, who won; J. D. Vance, who won; Blake Masters, whose race at this time is still undecided; and Joe Kent, whose race is also at this point undecided. [Both Masters and Kent ended up losing.] I would welcome a red wave of Republicans like them, who deserve to win. Maybe in 2024, there will be more candidates like them.

Third, the wrong kind of red wave would actually be bad for whites. Under Joe Biden, millions of whites have been radicalized. They now recognize that the Left is an implacable enemy committed to the degradation, dispossession, and ultimate destruction of white America. But they do not fully see what a weak and traitorous opposition the Republicans are. Thus, a red wave would have made these people feel safe again. It would have lulled them back to sleep. This would have allowed the Great Replacement to continue unabated, but under Republican leadership. But the failure of the red wave and the continuation of partisan gridlock will keep these white voters angry, agitated, and receptive to our message. That's the best possible outcome for White Nationalists.

The most plausible objection to my position is that even bad Republicans can be useful in culture war issues like abortion. For instance, without Mitch McConnell, Merrick Garland would be on the Supreme Court and *Roe v. Wade* would still be law. Setting aside the questions of whether or not Garland would be less dangerous on the Supreme Court than in the Justice Department, and whether the *Roe* victory aided or hindered Republicans at the polls, I just don't care about conservative culture war issues like abortion, trannies, or drag queens in libraries. Normie conservatives have those battles covered. Let them spend their political capital. We need to save ours for what matters most. Because if white people go extinct, I don't really care if the brown people who inherit the Earth have abortions or prayer in school. By the same token, if white people could be saved, I would not care if they were still fighting about abortion and other culture war issues a hundred years from now.

My greatest fear is not being ruled by crazed Leftists, since they can only hasten the end of this system. Instead, my worst nightmare is that Republicans will crack down on crime, improve the economy, focus on conservative culture war issues, and turn dissidents into pathetic, dog-like plan trusters—all while failing to halt the Great Replacement; indeed, while putting it on firmer footing. The only thing worse than Left-wing, multicultural chaos is an orderly, stable multiculturalism—which is precisely what Right-wing civic nationalists promise us.

That includes even the best Republicans. But we must be clear about our motives. I don't support such people because they ultimately want what we want. I support them because they might help us get what we want, in spite of themselves, for instance by injecting our issues into political debates and by supporting policies that interrupt white demographic decline. These are genuine steps forward, genuine victories, and unlike the accelerationists, I don't think we win by losing.¹ We only win by winning. Ultimately, though, we won't win with Republicans, because they simply don't care about white people, so they will not create or restore white homelands.² That task falls to White Nationalists.

If white Americans had a country of our own, we would of course support law and order, patriotism, and sound economic policies, as well as healthy families and sexual norms—precisely because they make a country stronger. When anyone publicly supports these values—even Republicans—we should of course give our verbal support. Sometimes we should even vote for them. But let's never lose sight of the fact that America is controlled by anti-whites. It is their system now. Until we can replace them, anything that makes their system stronger makes us weaker.

Counter-Currents, November 11, 2022

---

¹ Greg Johnson, "Against Accelerationism," in *The Year America Died*.
² Greg Johnson, "Restoring White Homelands," in *The White Nationalist Manifesto*.

TRUMP 2024:
A Bad Idea Whose Time Has Come

Victor Hugo famously said that nothing can stop an idea whose time has come. Unfortunately, that also applies to bad ideas. Daniel Patrick Moynihan reportedly quipped that affirmative action is a bad idea whose time has come. I feel the same way about Donald Trump's third run for the White House.

In 2015–2016, I was a fervent Trump supporter because he dared question the establishment dogma that economic globalization and immigration are good things. But, although Trump was successful in injecting nationalist and populist ideas into political debate, most of his policies came to naught because of a hostile establishment, political naïveté, and his own weak character.

By 2020, I supported Trump's reelection simply because he was better than Joe Biden. I had given up on the idea that Trump would do anything to stop the Great Replacement, but I thought that he would at least slow it down, which would give our movement more time to do something about it. As I predicted, Biden has accelerated white dispossession, but at least we can console ourselves with the fact that he has also accelerated the rise of white racial consciousness.

However, we are not going to win by losing, as the accelerationists think. Eventually, we will need actual political victories, principally on immigration. At this point, it is unclear if any prospective Republican presidential candidates will offer credible immigration reform.

What is clear, however, is Trump's record of failure on what for us should be the central issue. What's he going to do? Promise us a wall? Indeed, Trump's failure on immigration is so embarrassing that he will probably try to avoid the whole issue.

Trump won in 2016 on a national populist platform with the slogan Make American Great Again. By the 2018 midterms, he was a shadow of his former self, but when he floated the idea of ending birthright citizenship, I felt a shred of hope. By 2020, the swamp had consumed him.

In 2020, he ran and won again as a normie Republican with the slogan Keep America Great, as if he had spent the past four years keeping his promises and really had Made America Great Again.

Trump discovered that the American political establishment is fanatically opposed to any policies that would help preserve the white majority and our way of life. Eventually, he threw in the towel and took the path of least resistance. There's no opposition to giving favors to Jews and blacks, so he did plenty for them, including the flurry of shameful pardons he gave to Jewish swindlers and black rappers as he exited the White House, leaving the January 6th protestors to be tormented by his enemies.

Trump's midterm endorsements were a mixed bag. Some were good, like Vance and Masters, but others were terrible, like Herschel Walker and Mohammed Genghis Öz. What do these endorsements have in common? Commitment to nationalist and populist principles? That would explain Vance and Masters, but not Walker and Öz. In truth, the only thing these candidates have in common is that they buttered Trump up sufficiently to get his endorsement. Trump, in short, is an unprincipled egomaniac, and it would be very foolish to depend on him for anything.

Trump was worth a try in 2016. He was better than Biden in 2020. On a whim, Trump might say and do good things in the future. But at this point, it is silly to expect anything good from him.

Trump's speech announcing his candidacy was shockingly bland in content and low-energy in presentation, focusing on such traditional Republican themes as economics, law and order, and foreign policy, with precious little on immigration. Instead, Trump's main objections to the collapse of our southern border are now the flow of drugs and "human trafficking" rather than the flow of millions of migrants. The whole speech sounded like it was the product of many hands: pollsters, political consultants, and focus groups. But it was heavy on bragging and superlatives, which are definitely Trump's hucksterish touches.

What it lacked was the old Trump energy and the nationalist, populist red meat that put him in the White House in 2016. Is Trump trying to "normalize" himself? Is he counting on a backlash to put him into power? Backlash politics didn't produce a Red Wave in 2022, and it won't sweep Trump back into the White House in 2024.

I am old enough to remember how the hapless Bob Dole became the Republican nominee to save us from the Clintons in 1996. Did anyone, even Bob Dole, believe that he was the best candidate? Probably not. Did anyone think he was a particularly strong candidate? Again, probably not. Then how did he become the candidate? Why weren't people more willing to open up about their reservations?

Because, although nobody was particularly thrilled about Dole, he had "name recognition," and he had been around for a long time. So doesn't that mean that at least *some* people think well of him? He's been elected to the Senate, after all. Doesn't that mean he is "electable"? Besides, the most important thing is beating the other guy. We have to come together to beat the other guy. And isn't the other guy so terrible that we don't really have to come up with the best candidate? So why fight about the best candidate, when really any candidate will do?

Come to think of it, this is precisely how the Democrats ended up with Joe Biden as their champion in 2020. This is how bad ideas triumph.

The bad idea of Trump 2024 will be unstoppable only if people are willing to keep their reservations to themselves because they are intimidated by real or imagined opposition, or if they think that giving in to cynicism is the mature thing to do. Thus, it is important to create safe spaces where people can share their reservations about Trump and dream a little about what would constitute an ideal candidate. *Counter-Currents* is one such safe space.

The most widespread argument for supporting Trump in our circles now is that he would trigger the Left and further polarize the electorate. This is true. Another Trump campaign will certainly be destructive. It will also provide a lot of nihilistic entertainment for the extremely online. But this argument pretty much concedes that no pro-white policy victories can be expected from Trump. It is essentially an accelerationist position.

But, again, we will not get a white homeland with an ever-snowballing losing streak. We won't win simply by triggering and owning the libs. At a certain point, pro-white policies will have to win out. That's going to be a long journey, and the first step is to articulate pro-white policies and organize ourselves as a political bloc that politicians must cater to. We should begin that journey today.

Counter-Currents, November 17, 2022

Palestinians & Jews, Again

Once again, Palestinians and Jews on the shores of the Levant are demonstrating the worst feature of modern warfare: It solves nothing, because it seldom kills the people who are really at fault. In fact, neither side is really trying. Instead, they are gleefully killing innocents, while legions of morally demented bystanders frantically cheer them on.

The reason both sides target civilians is that their goal is ethnic cleansing through terror: Jews want Palestinian land, and Palestinians want Jewish land. Ultimately, the question is: Who has the *right*, the *just* claim, to the land? As an ethnonationalist, I believe that both peoples have the right to a land of their own *somewhere*, as long as it is not the same place, of course. (In my essay "The Autochthony Argument," I argue that it is more important that every people have a home *somewhere* than it is for them to have a home on their *original* territory, which is often impossible.[1])

When the Ottoman Empire was dismantled, it should have been partitioned into homelands for its constituent peoples: Turks, Greeks, Armenians, Kurds, Arabs and other Arabic-speaking peoples, and Jews. Of course, this did not happen, because the British and French empires preferred to grab what they could. Thus, everyone had to fight for an independent state. The result has been more than a century of bloody conflict.

If, however, the British and French had partitioned the Ottoman Empire along ethnic lines, the establishment of

---

[1] Greg Johnson, "The Autochtony Argument," in *Confessions of a Reluctant Hater*, 2nd ed. (San Francisco: Counter-Currents, 2016).

a Jewish state would have been seen as an anti-colonial, anti-imperialist act rather than the last gasp of European colonialism. (It didn't help that most Jews who "returned" to Israel came from Europe, not the Ottoman Empire, and were genetically about as European as they were Middle Eastern.)

From an ethnonationalist point of view, the only way for Jews and their Palestinian neighbors to live in peace is for both peoples to have sovereign homelands, which requires settling borders and forever relinquishing claims to one another's territories. That is what *should* happen. But it won't happen anytime soon, because neither side wants that, and the rest of the world enables their continued conflict rather than forces them to bury the hatchet.

So now that we have arrived at the realm of *Realpolitik*, let's talk about the current crisis. First, I have to be frank: My sympathy is with the Palestinians, because I, too, feel that I am part of a stateless people under a Jewish occupation regime. (For instance, I am censored on the largest social media platforms because an American Jewish organization, the Anti-Defamation League, thinks that freedom of speech is bad for Jews.) I certainly don't see the situation as Spencer Quinn does, with the Jews as white settlers and the Palestinians as savage Apaches.[2]

But feelings of sympathy don't go too far in the world of *Realpolitik*, because as much as I want a world in which all peoples—Palestinians, Jews, and Americans—live at peace in their own homelands, very few Palestinians or Jews reciprocate such sentiments. This is abundantly clear in the current conflict.

Again, both sides are targeting civilians because they are committed to ethnic cleansing through terror. Where do they want the refugees to go? Both sides are quite can-

---

[2] Spencer J. Quinn, "It's Not About the Palestinians," *Counter-Currents*, October 9, 2023.

did about this. Jews want to displace 3.5 million Palestinians to Europe and other white countries, and Palestinians want to displace more than seven million Jews to the same destinations. But that's bad for white people, because all white peoples are already in danger of losing our historic homelands to mass immigration and low fertility.

Why, then, are so many other White Nationalists cheering on the Palestinians?

The founder of Zionism, Theodor Herzl, believed that diaspora Jews came into conflict with their host populations because they had conflicting values and interests. His solution was to create a Jewish state. If a Jew accepts Herzl's analysis of the Jewish Question and his proposed solution, he is a Zionist. If a non-Jew like me wholeheartedly agrees with Herzl and wishes Jews the best in their own homeland, he is called an anti-Semite. But conflicts like this make me feel that there is a world of difference between me and fellow White Nationalists who are cheering for the destruction of Israel.

Yes, in the short term, such conflicts can't help but pull some Jewish manpower away from operations that harm whites, such as agitating against freedom of speech and for open borders. Yes, such conflicts are highly instructive to the general public when they see that the American political establishment is more concerned with Israel's borders than America's. Yes, the sudden normalization of bloodthirsty and bellicose nationalism and racial hatred against Palestinians in the mainstream media is also highly educational. But these are trivial boons given what is really at stake.

If Hamas has its way, more than seven million Jews will show up in our countries. Does any pro-white person really want that?

Of course, Hamas is not going to get its way. But these attacks raise the likelihood that instead white countries will have to absorb 3.5 million more Palestinians. How can any pro-white person cheer that on?

Of course, Hamas' cheerleaders aren't thinking that far ahead. They are just engaged in emotional self-indulgence. Unfortunately, the emotion they are indulging in is self-destructive. They are indulging in spite.

Spite means hating your enemies more than you love yourself. I can't help thinking that both Hamas and their White Nationalist cheerleaders are in the grip of spite. Pox Populi raises a very good question:

> As Israel retaliates against Hamas with "overwhelming force" and the approval of demented Zionists and Zionist toadies, I'm reminded of Machiavelli's words: "If an injury has to be inflicted on a man, it should be so severe that the man's vengeance need not be feared."
>
> I wonder what Hamas thought they would gain from this assault which, while large-scale relative to previous attacks, is still nowhere near a full-scale and debilitating attack. Surely they must have known that Israel would respond with all its fury.[3]

The answer is that Hamas is acting out of spite. They hate their enemies more than they love their own people, so they are eager to harm Jews, even to no earthly benefit. (It helps, of course, that Muslims believe they will be rewarded for suicidal attacks in heaven.)

When one recognizes that it seldom ends well when different peoples occupy the same territory, one has a choice. One can wallow in ethnic hatred, or one can seek a solution. My preferred solution is distinct homelands for distinct peoples. Other White Nationalists don't want Jews to live anywhere because they don't want them to live. I call them exterminationists. They are highly aroused

---

[3] https://t.me/pox_populi/7189

by the current conflict. But their position is indefensible.

No matter which side in this conflict wins, whites will lose. So if you ask me which side I am on, I am taking my own side, the white side. If white nations had pro-white governments, they would seek to resolve this conflict so that the Jewish and Palestinian diaspora populations on our shores could return to peaceful homelands, rather than grow through endless conflicts—conflicts that always have the possibility of igniting new regional or global wars.

Counter-Currents, October 11, 2023

ABORTION & WHITE NATIONALISM, AGAIN

"Never interrupt your enemy when he is making a mistake."

— Napoleon

Roe v. Wade, the US Supreme Court decision that legalized abortion throughout America has been overturned. This is the most significant victory by American conservatives since the end of the Cold War. Sadly, it is bad for white people.

If the Supreme Court throws out *Roe v. Wade*, this ruling means only that the US Constitution says nothing about the legality of abortion, thus the question must be determined by state legislatures, not the high court. If *Roe v. Wade* is overturned, however, many states will dramatically limit abortion.

I am of two minds about abortion.

On the one hand:

I believe that human life begins at conception, and human beings have a right to life. Having a right to life means simply: Human life is highly valuable, thus there is a *prima facie* case for preserving it, and you need a really good argument not to do so. Human rights mean that we need to arrange our affairs so that we respect the lives of others, even if it would be more convenient or profitable to rob, rape, or kill them. Fortunately, the world is big and rich enough to ensure every human being has a place.

There are, of course, circumstances in which people lose their right to life. If a man tries to kill you, you certainly have the right to use lethal force to protect yourself. People who commit heinous crimes arguably lose their right to life. Moreover, we should have no compunctions about killing enemy soldiers and spies if they are fighting against us.

But you must *do something* to lose your right to life. The only thing an unborn child can do to merit lethal force is to pose a medical threat to its mother's life, and that doesn't include merely upsetting her. But such circumstances only account for a tiny percentage of abortions.

Arguments for abortion on demand are a mountain of sophistries, dishonest euphemisms, and emotional manipulation.

Roe v. Wade is a terrible legal decision. Allowing it to stand for nearly half a century is a mockery of American justice.

Abortion advocates are among the most disgusting people in the world.

The people who choose to abort their children are generally trash and scum. At the very least, they are weak and selfish.

A decent society would ban abortion "on demand." Killing human beings is serious. Abortion should be treated as a form of execution. Thus if a woman wishes to seek an abortion, there should be a legal proceeding to determine whether the unborn child has, in effect, committed a capital crime. Both the child and its father have rights and should have representation in the proceeding. Under no circumstances, however, would a decent society treat abortion as merely a personal choice, with no more moral importance than cutting one's hair or trimming one's nails.

The pro-life movement should be a model for White Nationalism. Abortion, like white genocide, is a slow, cold genocide taking place in what seems like a normal society. Over 60 million abortions have taken place in America since *Roe v. Wade*. If a crime of such magnitude can be hidden from most people, then so can the even greater crime of white genocide. The pro-life movement's most important achievement has been simply awakening millions to the magnitude of the horrors happening invisibly all around us.

At the core of the pro-life movement is an enormous moral outrage and urgency. And yet the pro-life movement has been disciplined enough to rein in people who argue that resisting genocide requires acts of terrorism. If your goal is to shine a light on an invisible genocide against the innocent, then terrorist attacks that also inevitably harm the innocent are not the way to do it. They obscure rather than reveal the true crime of abortion, and they render both sides morally equal in the eyes of the public. White Nationalists need to take this lesson to heart as well.

On the other hand:

We don't live in a decent society. We live in a profoundly sick society, and we face a far bigger problem than abortion, namely white genocide. Because of low white fertility, non-white immigration, and policies that discriminate against whites in favor of non-whites, whites in America are in danger of biological extinction. Because all of these trends are predictable outcomes of social policies and could be remedied by better policies, white extinction is actually white genocide.

Legalizing abortion nationwide through *Roe v. Wade* is one of the few liberal triumphs that actually works in the demographic favor of whites. Currently, about 70% of women who seek abortions in America are non-white. Of the white women who seek abortions, surely some percentage is aborting non-white babies as well. That means that fewer than 30% of abortions are of white babies. Non-whites are massively overrepresented among abortion seekers, while whites are massively underrepresented. If *Roe v. Wade* had never been passed, there would be more whites and non-whites in America, but the non-white percentage of the overall population would be much larger, which means that the cultural and demographic decline of white America would be far more advanced, perhaps too far advanced to be reversed. Overturning *Roe v. Wade* while open borders, low white fertility, and anti-white discrimination remain in effect will only hasten white decline and make it harder to regain control of our own destiny.

One argument against abortion is that the people who choose to abort their children are usually trash and scum. But that's also an argument for it. Since trashy and scummy traits are heritable, giving such people access to abortion decreases their representation in future generations. *Roe v. Wade* is thus the only liberal triumph that has eugenic rather than dysgenic effects.

What, then, should be the White Nationalist position on abortion?

In a White Nationalist society, I would ban most abortions. However, this is not a White Nationalist society, and under present circumstances, we have bigger problems to deal with. Thus, if you think that white genocide is our greatest problem and White Nationalism is the solution, White Nationalists should not spend any of our scarce social, political, and financial capital opposing abortion. To do so is utterly irresponsible. It will simply hasten our own doom.

But if abortion works in our favor, should White Nationalists actively *promote* it?

Absolutely not.

It goes back to the question of human rights. I believe that White Nationalism is completely consistent with respecting the rights of other human beings. We can't just murder millions of people because it is convenient. That may be fine for liberals, but the New Right occupies higher moral ground.

By the same token, however, when we see our enemies (Leftists and non-whites) eagerly murdering millions of their own offspring, are we morally obligated to stop them, especially when stopping them hastens white genocide?

Absolutely not.

Saint Augustine famously prayed to God to help him be chaste and continent, "but not yet." That's the proper White Nationalist position on abortion. We should end it. But not yet.

Counter-Currents, May 5, 2022

IS IT RATIONAL FOR BLACKS TO DISTRUST WHITES?

Is it rational for blacks to distrust whites? Yes, absolutely.

Why is this important? If blacks and whites are to live together in a workable society, they must be able to trust one another. For instance, people of a classical liberal bent believe that a workable multiracial society is possible if people act as individuals and follow their rational self-interest. But this model fails if blacks have good reasons not to trust and cooperate with whites.

How do we understand and trust people of different races? We can't read their minds. So we have to listen to what they say and observe what they do. Based on what white people say and do, do blacks have a rational basis for trust and cooperation? The answer is no.

Some white people genuinely like blacks and treat them decently. An astonishing number of ordinary white people have the gut conviction that, as far as blacks are concerned, they are good, well-meaning, and trustworthy people.

But some of these nice white people quite freely condemn other whites as incorrigible anti-black racists. Sometimes, it is even true. Beyond that, some whites quite candidly declare that they dislike blacks. Between the whites who admit to being racist and the whites who condemn the racism of their fellow whites, blacks have ample reason to think that a significant number of white people bear them ill will and are thus not to be trusted.

Slavery ended a long time ago, but white supremacist laws were on the books in the United States within the lifetimes of many who are reading this essay. Leopards can't change their spots, but humans can change their minds. Few people today admit to being racists. But do people *really* change that fast? And is it prudent to assume that they have changed when something important is at stake?

Since it is not possible to tell good whites and bad whites apart simply at a glance, it is not rational for blacks to trust *any* whites—not even the whites who *say* they like blacks. After all, if white people are bad enough to hate blacks, aren't they also bad enough to lie about it? Even as explicit forms of racism and white supremacy have disappeared, don't white people say that blacks are still victimized by increasingly subtle and occult forms of implicit racism? Sure, racist macroaggressions like lynching are a thing of the past. But what about microaggressions so small that only experts can discern them? Don't nice white people like Robin Diangelo tell us that even nice white people like her are guilty of racism? Don't white experts now say that whites need not think bad thoughts about other races to be racists? It is merely enough for whites to *exist* to be racist. Blacks who internalize this message would be crazy to trust white people.

Nor is it rational for blacks to undertake the risks of trying to turn white strangers into white friends. Extending the hand of friendship always entails some risks. Taking that risk is only rational on the assumption that others are basically trustworthy and well-disposed toward you. But that assumption is precisely what is lacking between blacks and whites. So it is not rational for blacks to risk befriending whites, especially when it is far less risky to befriend their own kind.

Therefore, trusting whites, which is the foundation of any workable multiracial society, is simply not in the rational self-interest of blacks.

This argument is bound to provoke angry denials from white liberals and libertarians, who believe that a multiracial society really is workable. It is likely to spur them to new attempts to demonstrate their good will toward blacks, unlike those bad white people.

Such protestations are likely to be popular with blacks, because they usually involve free stuff, but they are also likely to be futile for two main reasons.

First, protesting yet again that one is unlike those bad white people over there simply underscores the existence of bad white people. Furthermore, it would not help white liberals to simply shut up about the existence of bad white people. There are enough outspoken white racists out there, so remaining silent about something so obvious is sure to cause distrust.

Second, offering free stuff to mistrustful blacks is self-defeating. It simply rewards them for being sullen, hostile, and suspicious, so why would they change their behavior? As long as whites are willing to pay blacks to establish their good will, blacks have massive economic incentives to dig up old grievances and invent new ones. Beyond that, nice white people have created a system in which blacks are babied, pandered to, placed above criticism, and literally allowed to get away with murder. Such a system gives free rein to blacks' worst impulses. It would make even the best of people into monsters.

White liberals believe, however, that after decades of soul-corrupting privilege and highly incentivized grievance mongering, blacks will become virtuous, open-hearted, trusting people like themselves. They'll decide to give up their racial privileges and lucrative rackets. They'll magnanimously descend from their pedestal. Then they'll finally be white people's equals.

White liberal outreach toward blacks has made race relations worse. Such measures can *only* make race relations worse. Yet white liberals continue to support such policies. Frankly, such self-defeating behavior should make blacks question not just the sincerity but the very sanity of whites who act this way—even as they queue up for more free stuff.

I really see no way around this problem. White racists and white anti-racists alike announce to blacks that a significant number of whites bear ill will toward blacks. Thus it is simply not rational for blacks to trust and cooperate with any given white stranger.

Of course, the same arguments for why it is not rational for blacks to trust whites also imply that it is not rational for whites to trust blacks. If white people had a country of our own, however, we would not have this problem. The same is true for blacks.

Counter-Currents, August 3, 2022

WHEN RICHARD HANANIA WROTE FOR *COUNTER-CURRENTS*

Richard Hanania is a rising star among Right-wing intellectuals. He has a J.D. from the University of Chicago and a Ph.D. in political science from UCLA. He first came to national attention in 2015 with an op-ed in *The Washington Post* about why Donald Trump was right not to apologize for his controversial remarks. (This is ironic, given recent events.) Hanania has gone on to publish at *The Wall Street Journal, National Review, Quillette, The American Conservative, Reason,* and *Palladium Magazine.* He was also a guest on *Tucker Carlson Tonight.* His book *The Origins of Woke* will be published this fall by HarperCollins. Hanania also runs a non-profit called the Center for the Study of Partisanship and Ideology from which he has drawn more than $100,000/year. But Hanania's primary platforms are Substack and Twitter, where he has substantial audiences.

I first took notice of Hanania in 2020. I was never a fan. He struck me as a libertarian who occasionally hinted at race realism, but then retreated to color-blind meritocracy and dark classical liberal mutterings about the dangers of collectivism and social engineering. I simply have no time for such foolishness. The white race is dying, largely through social engineering, and color-blind meritocracy or praying to the "invisible hand" or "spontaneous order" will not save us. We need white collectivism, state power, and pro-white social engineering.

But an astonishingly high percentage of American White Nationalists are ex-libertarians, so I took out a free subscription to Hanania's Substack to monitor him. Earlier this year, Hanania published an article entitled "Diversity Really is Our Strength," subtitled "Immigration destroys social cohesion. Good."[1] He has also inveighed against online anonymity. (Again, ironic, given recent events.) Gradually, I began to hate him.

It turns out, though, that Richard Hanania and I go way back, and I didn't even know it. From 2009 to 2011, I published Hanania under the pen name Richard Hoste, first at *TOQ Online* and then at *Counter-Currents*.

Hoste was a joy to work with. He was intelligent, versatile, prolific, wrote well, had interesting insights, and was enthusiastic about exploring ideas. He was also a prompt correspondent and never threw diva fits over editing.

Hoste's views on eugenics were too illiberal for my tastes. But he was 100% sound on the two litmus issues for writing for *TOQ Online*: He was a race realist, meaning that he believed in biological racial differences, and he was awake to the Jewish question. For instance, Hoste begins his essay "The Case for Group Selection: Its Deniers" with the words, "I'm not one to be suspicious of an intellectual just because he happens to be Jewish. But Emory University's Melvin Konner seems to be a character straight out of [Kevin MacDonald's] *The Culture of Critique*."[2]

At some point, I became aware that Hoste was a Palestinian Arab, but that did not alter the fact that he identified as a white man and wrote in defense of white interests. At a certain point, Hoste stopped writing because he wanted to focus on graduate school. I was sure he would do well. But I never heard from him again, not even a postcard.

Richard Hanania is not the only *Counter-Currents*

---

[1] Richard Hanania Substack, "Diversity Really Is Our Strength: Immigration destroys social cohesion. Good," June 10, 2023.

[2] Richard Hoste, "The Case for Group Selection: Its Deniers," *TOQ Online*, August 10, 2009.

alumnus to have an illustrious career as a more mainstream public intellectual. But he is the only one to have been doxed. Hanania began writing for Richard Spencer's *AlternativeRight.com* webzine in 2010. Spencer chose to use a third-party platform called Disqus for comments. In 2017 Disqus was hacked, and the emails and passwords of its clients were revealed. Antifa used Hoste's Disqus profile to reveal his identity.

AlternativeRight.com was not the only site in our sphere to use Disqus. It was also adopted by *The Right Stuff* (TRS) and *Radix Journal*. (Readers asked me to adopt Disqus at *Counter-Currents*, but I declined because it seemed an obvious security risk. I personally used it at other sites because I self-doxed a long time ago.)

Of course, I would never take the word of an antifa "journalist" that Hoste and Hanania are the same man. But Richard Hanania has now confirmed that he was Richard Hoste in an article entitled, "Why I Used to Suck, and (Hopefully) No Longer Do."[3] Actually, Richard Hoste was quite based. But Richard Hanania sucks big time, and this article only makes matters worse.

My first question is: Was Hanania lying about his purported "academic research" which showed that refusing to back down from controversial statements is a good strategy in garnering public approval? If it is true, why did Hanania not follow his own research?

Hanania characterizes the views he published at *Counter-Currents* and similar platforms as "repugnant" and renounces them. Beyond that, he says that he was not entirely in earnest. He was "trolling."

Sorry, but I am not buying it. Trolls post one-liners on social media. They do not read thousands of pages of densely-written academic works and write carefully-

---

[3] Richard Hanania Substack, "Why I Used to Suck, and (Hopefully) No Longer Do," August 6, 2023.

crafted multi-thousand-word reviews.

Richard Hanania is asking us to believe that the things he wrote under a pen name at White Nationalist and human biodiversity sites—including endorsing ideas from Kevin MacDonald's *The Culture of Critique*—were not entirely in earnest, but that the more moderate and socially acceptable things he wrote under his own name—when he was both subject to cancellation and rewarded with money and status—are actually honest and sincere. Only a fool would believe that.

The most charitable interpretation of Richard Hanania's career trajectory is that he remained race-wise and Jew-wise, but he edged up to the mainstream to inject good ideas and shift the Overton window.

He was wildly successful. Hanania is not just an intelligent and energetic writer. He's also an entrepreneur. He had a good thing going. So, when his real views were revealed, he panicked, cucked, and doubled down on the classical liberal, color-blind meritocracy cover.

It is a depressingly old pattern: smart libertarian and conservative nerds start noticing collectives, especially Jews and blacks, but as soon as there is a hint of pushback, they say, "But I treat everyone as an individual." Basically, they realize that this is a world of clashing tribes, in which individualism is a sucker's game. Then they get scared—because they have no tribe to protect them—and signal to the enemy tribes (almost always Jews), "I'm an individualist, so even though I *notice* collectives, I won't *act* on that knowledge. So you don't have to destroy me. You can just play me for a sucker."

I wish that Richard Hanania had not behaved in such a dishonorable way. There's more to this struggle than spreading ideas. There is also a moral component, and not just moral *ideas* but moral *character*. The Right has the truth on our side. But we've *always* had the truth on our side. We lose not for lack of truth, but for lack of courage.

Conservatives and libertarians have many good ideas. But they have weak guts. By cucking under pressure, Hanania reinforces the bourgeois cowardice that allows crazed Leftist fanatics to keep winning, even though they are intellectually bankrupt.

Truth alone will not set us free. All the truth in the world will change nothing if men lack the courage to stand by it.

Counter-Currents, August 7, 2023

Politics vs. Self-Help

White people face enormous challenges today.

Our living standards are declining due to globalization, immigration, and anti-white discrimination.

Our societies are being destroyed by multiculturalism, anti-whiteness, and the debasement of all standards: of behavior, of education, of taste.

Our private lives are in chaos as well. The collapse of norms governing sex has led to rampant confusion. Men and women don't know what to expect from one another, so it is increasingly difficult to form and maintain relationships, much less families.

This confusion has been compounded by online pornography and chatrooms, which have led to the proliferation of increasingly bizarre and boutique fetishes, including a shocking uptick in the number of transsexuals.

It is hard enough for ordinary people to find soulmates these days. Imagine the plight of a preop male-to-female who identifies as a dragon.

Unsurprisingly, all this real-world misery has driven increasing numbers of white people to despair. Thus we see rising levels of addictive forms of escapism, from relatively benign pastimes such as gaming to drugs, both legal and illegal. Drugs and nihilism are also leading to rising numbers of white "deaths of despair." Indeed, the average white lifespan is now shrinking, something that we associate with war or civilizational collapse.

No white person is immune to an anti-white system, but some of us are more vulnerable than others. For instance, working- and middle-class whites are more vulnerable to the effects of globalization and immigration than businessmen and professionals, some of whom actually benefit from such changes. Younger people are more vulnerable to the collapse of sexual norms than people who grew up in healthier times. Younger people are also more online and thus more susceptible to the poisons that spread there. Rich people actually abuse drugs and alcohol more than the poor, but they are also less vulnerable to the downward mobility that inevitably follows.

Thus it is harder for older and more prosperous whites to relate to the challenges of Millennials and Zoomers. This has led to a whole genre of hilarious "Okay, Boomer" memes in response to sincere but clueless advice on how to find a job or a mate. It has also led to bitter and borderline insane diatribes blaming entire older generations of whites for present problems.

As a White Nationalist, my aim is to promote white tribal consciousness based on an awareness of common identities, interests, enemies, and, yes, grievances. Once whites sufficiently collectivize, we can pursue political solutions to these problems: abolishing anti-white discrimination, de-globalizing our economic lives, halting immigration and commencing emigration, cracking down on the purveyors of addictive escapism, and restoring healthy families and sexual norms.

Why *political* solutions? Because ultimately, all the problems we face are political. What is happening to white people is not a mere "misfortune." It is not random. It is not natural. It is intentional and malevolent. These problems arise from political decisions whose predictable consequences are to make life increasingly difficult and finally impossible for whites. As individuals, we can do what we can to adjust to these problems. But the problems themselves will vanish only if we collectivize and take political action to remove them.

Of course we are going to face plenty of opposition, some of it from very close to home, some of it from within our own movement.

When faced with stories of fellow whites in distress,

you have the choice of being big or being small.

The big response is white solidarity based on shared blood, shared culture, shared enemies, and the recognition that we are all in this together. White solidarity is necessary for any sort of *political* solution to white decline; i.e., the *only* solution to white decline.

The "small" response to white decline is premised on individualism, which in turn is premised on a conviction of superiority, even invulnerability. This is delusional, because anti-white policies target us all. Such attitudes, moreover, prevent a political solution, which requires white solidarity. Indeed, such attitudes are so inimical to White Nationalism that our enemies would actively promote them if our "own" people did not do it for them.

The most common "small" response to white decline is to use it as an opportunity to signal one's feeling of superiority: "*I'm* not threatened by affirmative action. *I'm* not threatened by a competitive economy. *I'm* not threatened by strong women. So what's wrong with y*ou*?" Or: "*I* don't have trouble finding a woman. What's wrong with y*ou*?" Or: "Young people today lack the work ethic of my generation. Surely that's why things are harder for them."

Such signaling is at least plausible given the undeniable fact that people aren't equal. Some people really are better than others. So some people are more vulnerable to social decline than others. But it is delusional to think that anti-white policies won't affect all whites eventually. Moreover, although people aren't equal, all whites are *good enough* to enjoy a homeland of their own.

But the proper response to such one-upmanship is to reject the individualist framework it assumes. Individual preening and posturing cannot lead to collective political solutions to collective political problems. So the proper response is: "Maybe that's true. But it is beside the point. We won't solve these problems as individuals. We will only solve them as a group."

The most obnoxious "small" response to white distress is to declare that subjecting whites to inhuman conditions is actually a good thing, because it is somehow "eugenic." Bad economic conditions disproportionately affect those with low-skilled jobs, which means that we will have fewer people with those "low-skilled job genes" in the next generation. Involuntary celibacy hits "beta males" harder than "alpha males," so that means we will have fewer of those "beta-male genes" in the next generation. Feminism weeds out "cat-lady genes." All those deaths of despair weed out those with genes for depression and substance abuse. Ten years ago, before the epidemic of transsexualism, we never suspected how many "tranny genes" were in the population, but now, thankfully, those weeds are being dealt with as well. In fact, the people who are flooding our countries with rapists and killers, our streets with drugs, our culture with decadence, and our minds with poisonous ideas such as white guilt and feminism are actually doing us a favor.

Although I regard this position as absurd and contemptible, eugenics is based in fact. Genes do play a role in our economic and sexual success, as well as our susceptibility to drink, drugs, and bad ideas.

But not every problem is caused by genes. Moreover, those problems that have a genetic component need not be solved that way. It is especially absurd to think that social problems based on bad ideas can and should be solved on the genetic level. For instance, instead of positing "cat-lady genes" that can be weeded out genetically over how many generations, why not simply counter feminist brainwashing today?

If genes matter and ideas don't, why share ideas about genes? If one's ideas are determined by genes rather than observation and argument, then educating people about genetics is really beside the point.

The most charitable explanation for describing our anti-white regime as eugenic is that such people actually feel deep sympathy for the plight of fellow whites. But they feel so impotent to change it that they are grasping at the straw of eugenics to see something positive in an otherwise intolerable situation.

But I don't buy that. I have never seen eugenicists who argue that *they* should be weeded out of the gene pool. Thus I suspect we are just dealing with people who wish to signal their sense of superiority while the world burns. They are, however, deluded to think that they are invulnerable to what is coming for all of us.

But the main problem with embracing white decline as eugenic is not moral or factual, but *practical*. It is individualistic and thus cannot lead to any collective political solutions.

Another obnoxious individualist meme is to shame whites for complaining by likening them to blacks blaming white people for their problems. It's as if someone didn't open our borders, institute anti-white discrimination, debase our culture, and destroy our institutions. It's as if these problems have always been here.

The truth is that white people's lives have become *objectively* harder over the past 60 years due to politically-engineered decline. So white decline is not merely a matter of a victim "mindset." We really are victims. *Thus, white people have every right to blame the decline of our societies on those who are responsible.* Comparing our complaints to those of blacks, who fail despite being an objectively privileged group, is not just insulting, it is obscene.

The most seductive individualist arguments against white discontent use the language of self-help. Self-help arguments can be benevolent ("Clean your room, Bucko") or mean-spirited ("Learn to code"). But they, too, have some basis in fact. Ultimately, we all have room for improvement, and there's always something we can do to better ourselves. So am I really going to argue against self-help? Yes, I am.

I have no objection to self-improvement as such. I am always trying to better myself. In fact, I think that life is largely about becoming the best possible version of oneself. But since we are not just individuals but social beings, self-actualization also entails social and political commitments.

Self-help arguments become problematic when they become entangled with apolitical or anti-political individualism. I am happy to grant that individual problems often have individual solutions. But there are also collective problems that require collective solutions.

Moreover, self-help programs often boil down to becoming better adapted to the current world so that one can flourish in it. But what if the current world is unjust? Wouldn't becoming better adapted to an unjust world be a bad thing? If so, then "self-help" is actually self-ruin, and the best way to help oneself is to channel one's misery into overturning and replacing an unjust order. In such a context, telling Bucko to first clean his room is just an establishment deradicalization technique.

All these individualist ploys to dismiss or shame white grievances fail to grasp the real nature of the current system, which is simply anti-white. That means that it is stacked against all of us, not just the whites you look down on. No accommodation to such a system is possible, because if the system continues, no whites will flourish in the end.

American politics has a strong element of farce. Leftists control the commanding heights of society: politics, academia, the media, even big business. Yet, they posture as outsiders and plucky rebels. Meanwhile, the Republicans occupy a subordinate position in the system, yet posture as the party of the plutocratic establishment, the party of the "winners" and "strivers."

The farce is compounded when utterly marginalized pro-whites respond to the complaints of poor white people by gallantly defending the plutocrats who despise and deplatform them.

If complaining about our anti-white system prompts not solidarity but nineteenth-century advice to "pull yourself up by your own bootstraps" (a physical impossibility, by the way), people will naturally doubt the seriousness and sincerity of our pro-white populism. It is an added irony that such quintessential "Boomer memes" are coming from the mouths of Millennials and Zoomers.

Many White Nationalists are ex-libertarians and conservatives, so it makes sense that such anti-populist attitudes linger on. But these ideas really need to be purged. White Nationalism seeks state power to make life easier for *all* white people. In our society, one will not have to struggle heroically to lead a normal life. And those who do struggle heroically will do so unburdened and unopposed and thus reap their full rewards. If you recoil from this vision, you might still be a Republican.

Counter-Currents, September 29, 2023

Racial Solidarity & Moral Hazard

"... if you told me you were drowning
I would not lend a hand."

— Phil Collins

"We must all hang together, or, most assuredly, we shall all hang separately."

— Benjamin Franklin

Race-conscious whites believe that our race as a whole is too individualistic compared to other races. We would do well to cultivate a feeling of white solidarity and brotherhood. This sentiment should be even stronger among race-conscious whites, lest we offer the world the absurd spectacle of a movement that preaches white solidarity but in practice is polarized by sectarian wedge issues and petty personal rivalries.

But we must be careful here. Too much solidarity can be a bad thing. For instance, we all recognize that black solidarity with their own criminals is pathological. Blacks regard law and order as alien and "white," which is true. Thus they stigmatize "snitching" on black criminals to the police. They also riot when black criminals like Trayvon Martin, Michael Brown, Ahmaud Arbery, George Floyd, etc. have unhappy encounters with law enforcement or armed victims.

This behavior makes it easier for black sociopaths to get away with crimes. In fact, the black sociopaths' advocacy group known as Black Lives Matter has been so successful at discouraging police from patrolling black neighborhoods and arresting black criminals that black crime is now soaring. Black criminals generally choose black victims. Thus many blacks are paying with their lives for their mindless solidarity with black criminals. Black solidarity with their own criminal element is a form of self-destructive spite. It seems that blacks hate white people, especially white cops, more than they love themselves.

If you make wrongdoing safer, you'll get more of it. This is the meaning of "moral hazard." Usually, moral hazards involve forcing other people to pay the costs of an individual's bad decisions. For instance, if the government bails out lenders, they will take more risks. Obviously, a well-run society creates incentives to reduce rather than increase bad decisions. The same is true of a well-run movement. This is why we must be careful of appeals to solidarity.

Unconditional solidarity with the wrongdoers among us is a moral hazard.

We should not extend unconditional solidarity to race-conscious whites who harm other members of our movement. These harms can range from promoting bad ideas and having bad manners—which should be called out and criticized, preferably with better ideas and better manners—to treasonous behaviors like doxing and snitching to our enemies, to outright criminal behavior. If solidarity is important to us, then we should feel solidarity with the victims.

Nor should we extend unconditional solidarity to whites—whether movement members or "normies"—who harm other members of our race at large. There are misanthropes in our cause who don't "love white people." They look upon white "normies" merely as raw material for their megalomaniac fantasies. But they'll still appeal to normies for white solidarity when it is convenient. Even a whiff of such sociopathic elitism is deadly for a populist movement. If solidarity is important to us, then we should reserve it for the vast majority of decent white people, not anti-social misfits who prey upon them.

Finally, we should not extend unconditional solidarity to whites who commit crimes against other races, for instance, terrorists like Brenton Tarrant. Even our enemies have basic human rights. But even if you deny that—even if you profess to care only about white people—whites like Tarrant also harm our movement and our race as a whole.

It is, of course, natural to feel greater affinity with race-conscious whites than for "normies" or non-whites. But we cannot lose sight of our larger goal. The purpose of white identity politics is to secure the existence and well-being of our race as a whole. That is the standard by which we must judge one another. And when a conflict emerges between members of our cause and white well-being as a whole, solidarity with our race as a whole should win out. We must always choose the greater good.

Now let's apply this to some concrete questions from readers. First, in response to an article criticizing Nick Fuentes,[1] one reader cited Benjamin Franklin's remark when signing the Declaration of Independence that "We must all hang together, or, most assuredly, we shall all hang separately." Second, a reader asked whether people in the movement should "bury the hatchet" and pull together to support the white advocates who have been targeted for lawfare for participating in Unite the Right in 2017. A third reader wants to help Jason Kessler's defense in the Charlottesville trial, but he regards some of the other defendants as bad people, to whom he wouldn't lend a hand even if they were drowning. He wonders if helping Kessler is right if it also helps bad people in the process. All three of these issues are related to the question of solidarity and moral hazards.

---

[1] Aquilonius, "Is America First Cracking Up?," *Counter-Currents*, September 23, 2021.

Let's deal with the Fuentes question first. Nobody in the movement is above criticism for bad ideas, bad decisions, or bad character. Suppressing criticism in the name of solidarity creates a moral hazard. It creates an atmosphere in which bad ideas, bad decisions, and bad characters flourish. But we can't afford that. Our cause is too important, our enemies are too powerful, our ranks are too small, and our time is too short.

However, when people like Fuentes are attacked by our enemies for being courageous and effective in advocating sound ideas—for instance, when he was deplatformed from Twitter and YouTube—then of course we should give him moral support at the very least. In such a case, doing nothing would itself create a moral hazard, since it would both decrease the likelihood of right action in our quarters and encourage wrongdoing among our enemies.

There were plenty of problems with Unite the Right. There were some terrible people, terrible ideas, and terrible optics. I know what is coming in the trial. I know that we will cringe with embarrassment at the testimony, depositions, emails, forum posts, and text messages that will be offered as evidence and broadcast to the entire world.

But that does not alter the fact that the Unite the Right marchers were there to exercise their constitutional rights—and that their rights were denied by a criminal conspiracy involving the city of Charlottesville, the Commonwealth of Virginia, and a constellation of Leftist groups including the domestic terrorists known as "antifa." The police allowed antifa to attack the Unite the Right marchers to create a pretext for stopping the event. All the violence and injuries at Unite the Right, including the death of Heather Heyer, were the consequences of the conspiracy to deny the Unite the Right marchers' constitutional rights. Unite the Right's participants were not attacked because of what you or I might deem bad ideas, optics, or character. They were attacked for being racially conscious whites taking a public stand against our erasure.

The same is true of the post-Charlottesville lawfare directed at the march's organizers and participants. They are not being attacked for what you and I might reject about their ideas and behavior, but for the things that we all agree with. Thus, the attack on them is an attack on all of us. So we all need to fight back. Thus, we should set aside our differences—since those don't really matter here, anyway—and we should offer them moral support, at the very least.

As the trial progresses, some of the defendants will make us proud. But we will also be confronted with statements, actions, and personalities that we cannot defend and that you will be asked to disavow. But hold the line. It is not illegal to be evil-minded fantasists and foul-mouthed jerks. It is not illegal to be an asshole. All the defendants, good and bad, are on trial simply for being white advocates. Make very clear that your support is not a blanket endorsement of the marchers—how could it be?—but simply a defense of their constitutional rights, as well as the basic principles of white racial activism, namely that white people are under attack, and we have the right to take our own side. On these points, at least, Unite the Right did nothing wrong.

Just as solidarity with wrongdoers within our ranks creates a moral hazard, so does a lack of solidarity when our people are persecuted for doing the right thing. If we use such attacks as occasions to air internal grievances rather than to pull together and counterpunch, we will simply encourage more sleazy legal harassment. Thus I wish the Charlottesville defendants the best. If they win, our cause will be a bit safer from lawfare. If they lose, we can only expect more of the same.

Counter-Currents, October 18, 2021

Revolution with Full Benefits

Jason Kessler recently offered a critique of the White Nationalist movement on his Telegram channel: "If White Nationalism is totally devoid of single White women and cannot provide basic social networking functions for single men, it is unsustainable." Indeed, White Nationalism is "worthless" because it "isn't providing basic social functions for its adherents," particularly providing men with mates.

I do not wish to discuss Jason Kessler or the broader phenomenon of "incels" (involuntary celibates). Suffice it to say that Jason Kessler is a dedicated white advocate and has my complete sympathy.

Instead, I want to deal with the question of the *benefits* people can expect from the White Nationalist movement. Is it reasonable to expect the movement to provide you with personal fulfillment, romantic or otherwise?

White Nationalism is a political movement. Like all political movements, we promise significant benefits. Indeed, we promise enormous, world-shaking changes. We promise to reverse the demographic, cultural, and political decline of the white race, through creating or restoring sovereign homelands for all white peoples.

Reversing our demographic decline does entail rolling back the so-called sexual revolution, which, similar to the Bolshevik revolution, promised freedom and plenty but ended up delivering a dystopia in which increasing numbers of young people lead lonely, sexless lives. So yes, White Nationalism promises an end to the incel problem.

But all of that comes *after* we win.

In the meantime, we face enormous opposition. Our people have been brainwashed into self-loathing and self-destruction. And when people do wake up, the entire establishment will spare no expense and sink to any infamy to crush dissent and hold on to power. Then there are the retarding effects of antiquated ideologies, aberrant personalities, anti-intellectualism, and self-defeating behaviors in our own ranks.

Despite all of these hindrances, our movement is growing. But compared to our rivals—and compared to what our movement needs to be if we are to beat them—White Nationalism is still a small, poorly-organized, and poorly-equipped vanguard. But great things can come from small beginnings.

But if you want to join this vanguard today, *you should not be asking what the movement can do for you but what you can do for the movement.* This is the ethos which will build a movement that, someday, will be able to deliver benefits, not just to its members but to our race as a whole.

I am not saying that there are no emotional rewards in this fight, that it is all self-sacrifice, and that you will never find happiness along the way. But your happiness can't be our movement's primary concern—indeed, it shouldn't even be *your* primary concern—for two principal reasons.

First, happiness falls into the category of "outcomes"—i.e., things produced by action. Every political movement is about outcomes. In our case, we want to save our race. Compared to that collective good, individual happiness is just not that important. This movement is not about meeting our personal needs. This is politics, not therapy. At this stage of the struggle, we need people who are more focused on *giving* to the movement rather than *taking* from it. That's simply the only way we will build a movement that can someday deliver benefits—including greater individual happiness—to our race as a whole.

Second, there are some things we can control and some things that we can't control. Discerning the difference is the beginning of wisdom. Happiness depends on circumstances we can't control, and when you are a dissident, you have enemies working constantly to deny you those circumstances.

We can, however, control the principles we stand for and the goals we strive to achieve. If we choose good principles and goals, and strive to the best of our ability to achieve them, some of their goodness rubs off on us. We become *worthy* of praise and *worthy* of happiness. And even if circumstances don't work out to actually make us happy, we can take solace in the fact that we are at least *worthy* of happiness.

Because we have more control over our worthiness to be happy than happiness itself, our primary concern should be our worth rather than our happiness. Furthermore, happiness tends to show up anyway when you occupy yourself with more worthwhile pursuits. Happiness is like sleep: It comes naturally if you just let it happen, but it eludes you if you focus on it or grasp for it.

You can, moreover, simply *choose* to focus on your worth rather than your happiness. In fact, you can choose to do this *right now*. If you choose to fashion yourself into such a person, you will become a better activist, because you will not be tempted to quit due to personal problems and setbacks. Thus, you will be more likely to contribute to good collective outcomes in the long run.

There are plenty of opportunities for activism, which brings us back to Kessler's point about "basic social functions." We don't just need political activists. In fact, since political activism is increasingly repressed, nationalists have every reason to focus on other forms of community organizing.

White Nationalists in every community can create their own self-help and mutual aid groups. We need hiking and camping clubs, fitness and martial arts groups, book clubs, Toastmasters-style groups to develop communications skills, homeschooling networks, men's and women's groups, and family-friendly gatherings. We especially need organizations to help nationalists with drug and alcohol problems.

Such groups can serve as small-scale models of the kind of society we want to create for all white people. If we can't create good groups on a small scale, why would anyone trust us with whole societies?

Sure, you'll face opposition and hurdles. But other groups have overcome them, so you can, too—especially with their help. If you start such groups, though, you must be realistic: You will put more into them than you will get out of them, especially at the beginning.

It is silly to sign up at the beginning of a revolutionary struggle and expect a full package of benefits to go along with it. There will be many lean years ahead before we win. Our movement is more likely to benefit our race if we stop worrying about benefiting ourselves.

Counter-Currents, March 27, 2023

Thinking of Quitting the Movement?

The core of this article was published in 2017. The occasion was the cyberbullying of several female video commenters who eventually left the movement. The article was republished in the first edition of my book *Toward a New Nationalism*. I dropped it from the second edition, because the figures it referenced are no longer relevant. But the central arguments remain as relevant as ever. Thus I decided to remove any dated references and make it more perennial in tone.

Many people leave the White Nationalist movement because of endemic drama, including online bullying by obnoxious people. I favor an easy entry, easy exit policy. But you should have good reasons for leaving. Here are some reasons not to go.

Everyone in this movement inevitably finds himself wondering, "If the cause of White Nationalism is so good, why are the people so bad?" But we have to remind ourselves: "Despite the fact that the people are so bad, the White Nationalist cause still remains good." (I am paraphrasing an argument from Harold Covington.) The point is to see that, ultimately, the core of the movement is an idea, not a set of people. The people are there just to serve the idea, and that includes us.

REMEMBER THAT THIS CAUSE RUNS ON IDEALISM.
Whenever your enthusiasm for the cause wavers, remind yourself that you are doing this because, first and foremost, you think this is *right*. White Nationalism is about putting the common good of our race over individ-

ual interests whenever they conflict. That includes *our own interests*. A true idealist also acts out of duty rather than personal pleasure, whenever the two conflict. Yes, this cause is often joyful, and a successful movement has to offer personal rewards and pleasure. But in the last instance, we do what we do because it is right, not because it is fun. Which is how we stick to it when it isn't fun.

None of us may live to see free white homelands. So our activism is, at its core, sacrificing ourselves for the common good, for the future of our people. There's a saying that a society becomes great when people plant trees so their descendants can enjoy shade. White Nationalism is about creating a world in which our race has a future, even if we do not share in that future.

But we can share its greatness today. And that greatness shines most brightly when we endure the hard times, sustained by idealism alone. Of course the movement has to offer more than idealism and sacrifice. But they are the bedrock upon which it is built, and it will fail without them. Our race dies a little every time we choose self-indulgence over duty, the present over the future, private interests over the common good.

No, the idea cannot triumph without attracting good people. And every bad person who clings to this cause repulses a hundred better ones. So we have to understand why there are so many bad people and figure out ways of attracting better ones. But the White Nationalist idea is absolute. The people are fungible, and if good people are quitting while stupid, crazy, and evil ones are running amok, the movement is going to fail. When decent people listen to their feelings of disgust and start thinking of quitting, they are letting the bastards win.

You can't do that. You've got to listen to your idealism instead, and you also need to turn up your disgust a notch. If someone is behaving in a manner so disgusting that you are thinking of abandoning all that is good and holy, perhaps you should feel a bit disgusted with yourself as well.

Beyond that, if someone is disgusting enough to drive you from the battle, aren't they also disgusting enough for you to want to crush them? Because that's the spirit we need.

Of course, once you go beyond the beatific vision of crushing your enemies and ask yourself exactly how it can be accomplished, it dawns on you that *we can't really get rid of these people*. We can't kill them. We can't throw them in prison. We can't get them off the Internet. We can't track down all their donors and supporters. We can't shame and silence every shill. We can't revoke some sort of membership in the movement. We can't "purge" them.

But they can't do that to us, either.

White Nationalism is a decentralized, pluralistic, largely virtual movement. There are plenty of cliques and groupuscules and scenes. But there is no absolute inside and outside. There is no king, pope, or dictator. No arbiter of who is in and who is out. We can't even rid this movement of doxers, embezzlers, con artists, miscegenators, drunkards, druggies, chronic failures, and controlled opposition. But somehow, some of us have made a science of driving away decent people. That must stop. The closest thing we can do to purging all the bad elements is simply to leave them alone. Let them have their little cliques and cults. Let them serve as an abscess into which all the poisons drain.

RECOGNIZE THAT ALL THE POWER IS IN YOUR HANDS.

Nobody can make you leave this movement. Only you can do that. So don't.

If only you can make you leave the movement, *your enemies depend entirely upon you to hand them a victory.* Which makes bullying extremely stupid. Nobody can remain a leader for long if he fails repeatedly. That goes for online lynch mobs as well as political movements. The best way to avoid failure is to choose goals that you can actually accomplish. The more the outcome depends on your actions and the less it can be controlled by your opponents, the greater the chance of success.

In the case of bullying, however, success depends *entirely* on the victims. If the targets of bullying just hold firm, they win, and their enemies look incredibly weak and foolish. This sort of strategic stupidity is why the movement keeps lurching from one self-induced defeat to another.

MANAGE YOUR EXPECTATIONS.

There will never be a movement without destructive infighting, and it is unreasonable to expect otherwise. Even if we could convert or drive out the worst elements in the movement, the establishment that opposes us would simply create replacements. In short, these people—whether they know it or not, whether they intend to or not—are doing the enemy's work. Their goal is to create a smaller, weaker, poorer, more marginal, but "purer" movement—a movement with a madhouse atmosphere that repulses the normal and the superior—a movement that has zero chance of resonating with the masses, changing the course of history, and saving our race from extinction.

Well, that is the goal of our enemies as well. So if the troublemakers did not exist, the enemy would find it necessary to create them. Note that I am not accusing anyone of being an enemy agent. I am actually accusing them of being something far more contemptible: people who do the enemy's work for them, for free. Their motives ultimately don't matter. Controlled opposition or not, the results are exactly the same.

But if these people will always be with us, then they cannot constitute an argument for quitting, for then the movement will simply fail. Indeed, they only constitute an argument for working harder.

REMEMBER WHO YOUR REAL ENEMIES ARE.
Imagine that it were possible to completely extirpate movement infamy. If you try it, you will discover that it will quickly consume all your time and energy and prevent you from being able to do any positive work.

But our positive work is what will change the world, and we cannot let ourselves be deflected from it.

Ultimately, the best way to defeat one's opponents is simply to ignore them and focus on making constructive contributions to the movement. Always remember that we are in the business of slaying dragons, not swatting flies.

COUNT YOUR BLESSINGS.
I love this cause, and even with all the bad aspects, I would not trade my life for anything. As I put it in one of my essays:

> There have been times when I wished that I had never gotten involved with White Nationalism. I tend to focus on the negative and forget about the positive. Sometimes I brood over the fact that the craziest, crookedest, most loathsome people I have ever encountered have been White Nationalists—forgetting that the finest people I know are White Nationalists as well.
>
> My complaining finally angered a good friend, a secret agent who does as much as he can for the cause. He told me that I lead an enviable life, that I work full-time for the most important cause in the cosmos, that I can speak the truth as I see it for the rest of my days. Then he reminded me of the basic premise of *Buffy the Vampire Slayer*: Buffy has super-powers and is part of a secret initiatic society

doing battle with the forces of evil. Night after night, she is literally saving the world. And yet . . . all she wants to be is an ordinary high school cheerleader.

Well, when you put it that way, I choose to fight evil and save the world.[1]

DON'T ALLOW YOURSELF TO BURN OUT.
Even though idealism and self-sacrifice must, in the last instance, be what sustains this movement through the trials, if life were nothing but trials we would burn out and become useless to the cause. So do everything you can to build personal rewards into your activism. Above all, do not let yourself become isolated. Cherish the good people and do everything you can to avoid the bad ones.

UP YOUR EMOTIONAL INTENSITY.
I am haunted by W.B. Yeats' lines in "The Second Coming":

> The best lack all conviction, while the worst
> Are full of passionate intensity.

Other things being equal, this differential alone will be enough to bring any movement to ruin.

DON'T LOSE TRACK OF WHAT'S REALLY IMPORTANT.
The substance of our movement is its goal: creating free homelands for all white peoples, which is how I define White Nationalism. You are "in" our movement if you *fight for* that goal. Everything else that we *fight about* is a side issue.

Counter-Currents, October 25, 2023

---

[1] Greg Johnson, "In My Grandiose Moments . . .," *Truth, Justice, & a Nice White Country,* p. 234.

How to Leave the Movement

What do you do if you believe that nothing in the world is more important than White Nationalism—that we are not just fighting for our race's survival, but for all that is good and holy; indeed, for the very survival of life on Earth—and then you want to leave? Given the importance of the cause, you'd need a pretty good reason to quit, right?

But what if you want to leave to focus on your education, family, and career? What if you are just burned out and need a break? What if you are tired of dealing with pathological personalities and personal betrayals? What if you are leaving because you just don't see how your engagement is accomplishing anything? Don't these reasons seem selfish and trivial by comparison to the cause?

In my opinion, all of these are perfectly good reasons to take a break from movement activity or leave it altogether. But honestly, although you should have good reasons for everything you do, you don't need to *share* your reasons with me. You don't need my permission to leave. You can always leave *no questions asked*.

But you should *say something*, because if you just go silent, your friends and comrades will be worried about you. It is demoralizing when people just disappear.

What does it mean to say that you can come and go from the most important movement in the world, *no questions asked*?

First, we need to talk about what being part of our movement really means. Since the movement is largely online propaganda, the most minimal sense of "joining" or "leaving" is simply logging on to consume online propaganda, and then logging off again. There are plenty of people who don't want you to read my work. But you don't need my permission to log in or out of our online spaces.

If you want to join different movement groups, of course, you will find entry and exit to be more difficult.

Can you help the movement by doing nothing but consuming online propaganda? Yes, you can.

Ideas matter. By reading *Counter-Currents*, you are changing your ideas, and eventually that will change your behavior. And if enough people do that, we can change the course of history.

But in the meantime, even if you are merely passively consuming "content," you are helping. By reading our sites, you are generating "clicks" that help other people find the sites through search engines. At *Counter-Currents*, we also sell advertising, which helps us stay online. People pay us just on the chance that you will do something more than just passively consume information.

For every thousand people who visit this site, maybe a hundred of them do something more than simply read articles or listen to podcasts. They might share a link, post a comment, or click on an advertisement.

Some comments are profound. Some are dumb or annoying. But even an anodyne comment that nobody responds to can help foster a sense of community and boost people's morale.

For every thousand people who visit this site, one of them will actually send money to it through a donation or book purchase.

I don't know how many of our readers do anything in the movement IRL ("in real life"). But we are betting that the ideas you encounter here will influence your life in countless ways, from your conversation topics to your choice of a movie, a career, or a mate. If you see the world differently, you will act differently.

I would be delighted if, of the more than two million unique visitors who came to *Counter-Currents* in 2023, more than 200 of them will actually attend *Counter-Currents* events.

Now, before you start thinking that the numbers are stacked against us, let me just say that the numbers have always been stacked against every radical political movement. But small, organized minorities have made revolutions before. Indeed, they are the *only* force that makes revolutions. The masses are always moved and steered by minorities.

Beyond that, these numbers are actually good, so first and foremost, I am grateful. But these numbers can also get better, so after I thank you, I want to encourage all of you to do more.

I am not, however, going to insult, badger, bully, or gaslight you—for the simple reason that I think our movement will grow best if we all allow each person to choose his own level of involvement and respect such decisions, while gently reminding everyone that we need to do more if we are going to win. Indeed, the idea that people can come and go, no questions asked, is just one implication of respecting people's decisions about their level of commitment.

Let's dispense with the idea that being part of the movement is an all-or-nothing proposition. If you are thinking of quitting, why not consider taking a vacation or cutting back instead? If you are thinking of quitting, why not just quit one group and join another instead?

There are movement groups that model themselves on boot camps, cults, or totalitarian political parties. These groups try to make it very hard to quit. They frame it as an all-or-nothing proposition. This doesn't prevent people from quitting, of course. It just ensures that they quit in a noisy way, which makes it less likely for new people to join.

If movement membership is either all or nothing, more people are going to choose nothing rather than all. Thus it is self-defeating to frame things in this manner.

For many people today, being a White Nationalist is merely one more "extremely online" lifestyle, all of which have addictive aspects, which make them very difficult to quit. If your participation in the movement becomes an addiction, then it really does become an all-or-nothing choice. Again, this doesn't prevent people from quitting. It merely ensures that they quit in a wrenching and permanent manner.

How, then, can we avoid turning the movement into just an online addiction?

This movement should not be your life. The movement is a more-than-full-time job for me, and still it is not my entire life. I have non-political friends and pastimes. If I didn't, I would have burned out a long time ago. If you believe nothing is more important than serving our cause, you still need to take time off, or you will become useless to the cause.

Now let's run through some of these supposedly trivial reasons for leaving. Again, as far as I am concerned, you need not give me any reasons. But if you were to give me these reasons, I would say the following, then respect any decision you make.

First, you want to focus on your family, education, and career. That is laudable. But if you feel that you need to leave the movement to do these things, you are mistaken. Even if you think that nothing is more important than the cause, the cause itself is served best by people who are well-rounded and excellent in all walks of life. If you lead an exemplary life, you will attract people to the movement, strengthen it, and ensure that you are in it for the long haul.

Political commitment should never be an excuse for a stunted and disordered life. If you need to scale back your commitments or take a break to work on yourself, you *are* working for the cause.

Second, you are burned out and need a break. Thank you for your service. Take a break and come back when you feel better. But in the future, to prevent burnout, you might want to strike a better balance between the movement and other aspects of your life. If you can't bring yourself to do that for yourself, try doing so for the cause.

Third, you are tired of pathological people. I get it. But the entire movement does not consist of pathological people, so maybe you just need to associate with a better crowd.

Fourth, your engagement is not accomplishing anything. Even though you can help by merely consuming online content, even though you can also help by mere "shitposting," you still don't *feel* like you are accomplishing anything. It feels empty and pointless, a waste of time. Perhaps you yearn for IRL activism, especially group activism, but you are frustrated by the absence of political opportunities and by state repression of such groups.

My first thought is that maybe you should not quit but instead simply consider doing different things that are more productive or satisfying. My second thought is not to quit but to take time off to work on other aspects of your life. If there are no outlets for group activism at present, then consider focusing your efforts on self-improvement, mutual aid, or just enjoying one another's company. Again, a movement that requires accomplished, well-rounded individuals should encourage such groups. And if political opportunities present themselves, you will have a tight network already in place that can spring into action.

If you make it difficult for people to change their levels of commitment, they will simply quit. If you make it difficult for people to take breaks, they will simply quit. If you make it difficult for people to quit, they will engineer dramatic breaks.

I have seen a lot of exits from the cause over the years,

especially after Charlottesville. These exits have been either freely chosen or forced by circumstances like doxing. They have either been quiet or dramatic.

I believe that many of the dramatic exits took place because the person in question could not allow himself to just take a break for personal reasons.

If you believe that you can only leave our world-shaking and momentous cause for something even more world-shaking and momentous, you have a strong motive to feign some sort of dramatic conversion to a new worldview. Religious forms of apostasy are particularly attractive because there is a taboo on questioning their sincerity. I don't subscribe to that taboo. In my book, the only bad reason for quitting White Nationalism is a conversion, real or feigned, to an anti-white worldview.

If the movement is an all-consuming cult or an addiction, then you can't just take a break. You've got to wrench yourself away from it. If you want the break to be irrevocable, you will do something unforgivable. Thus I have encountered people who have engineered bitter personal breaks, betrayed good people to the enemy, and even race-mixed—all because they couldn't allow themselves to just take a sabbatical.

This is why I am convinced that we will actually recruit and retain people better by being easygoing about entry and exit.

Counter-Currents, April 4, 2023

Turning the World Around

Our friend Gaddius Maximus recently ran a series of revealing polls on his Telegram channel, *Building a Third Force*. The upshot of his polls is that most respondents believe, quite accurately, that our ideas have made enormous progress in the last few years.

But when he asked the final question, about whether people are more optimistic about our prospects, it was clear that even though most respondents saw great intellectual progress, they were not as sanguine about our actual political prospects. As one commenter put it: We have made a lot of intellectual progress, but society is objectively worse.

I think this might help explain the "movement malaise" people have been commenting about since the beginning of 2022.

Part of that malaise is merely a problem of optics. From the audience, it looks like the movement is shrinking because there are fewer people on stage, which is true. Many have closed up shop. But those of us on stage can see that there are more people in the audience than ever before, and by some indications, half of you have arrived here since 2018. Individual pundits may come and go, but our ideas are here to stay, and their impact is only growing.

But another part of the malaise is simply due to unrealistic expectations. Politics is downstream from culture . . . way downstream. Today's political events are the products of bad ideas that have been spreading for decades, even centuries. Our enemies have a huge head start. It takes time for a change of public consciousness to produce a change of policy—especially because the people in power will do everything they can to maintain their power in the face of rising opposition. And once we actually start influencing policy, we will encounter both active opposition and institutional inertia. But we know we can turn the world around because our enemies did it before us. Thus we can put things right.

We are like the passengers of an ocean liner. We see that the ship is heading full-steam toward an iceberg. But most of the passengers want to have fun, not listen to bad news, and the Captain and crew simply dismiss us as "iceberg haters" who lack faith in their leadership and their wondrous new machine. As the peril grows closer, more people will listen to us. Eventually, some of the crew might listen, too. Maybe the Captain will change course. Maybe the crew will mutiny and change course. Maybe the passengers will storm the bridge and change course. Even when the tide turns in our favor, we will still be hurtling toward disaster. Even when the course is finally changed, it takes a long time to turn a steamship. Even if one cuts the engines, inertia will speed it on toward doom. Even if the course is changed in time, things will continue to get worse—or at least look worse (the iceberg will loom larger)—before they get better.

Right now, we are still at the stage of awakening the passengers and crew. We know that things won't end well for the people on the bridge. An unsustainable course won't go on forever. But we don't yet know if it will end badly for the rest of us. Duty compels us to try to save the whole ship. Prudence dictates that we know where the lifeboats are. Realism tells us that things will get worse before they get better. But we must not give in to fear, because we will only win if we keep fighting.

Counter-Currents, July 7, 2023

Reasons for Optimism

There's a lot of bad news right now, and it is bound to get worse. But are there reasons for hope?

There are two kinds of optimism: irrational and rational. I am a constitutional optimist, which is the irrational kind. Thus I have to constantly ask myself if there really are good reasons for optimism for our cause and our people. The answer is yes. These are the reasons I come back to again and again.

First, we have the correct views of human nature and politics, which will allow us to better secure the goods of political life: identity, prosperity, security, peace. That is, *if* we gain power. But is there good reason to think that we will eventually gain power? That depends in part on our enemies and in part on our movement.

Second, the current political establishment is premised on falsehoods about human nature and politics that can only lead to disaster. The big question is not *"Will* they lose power?," but *"When* will they lose power?" There's also a question about *how* they will lose power. Will they destroy the world, or will sane people take over before then? Again, that depends in part on our enemies and in part on us.

Third, our movement is growing, and I don't just mean White Nationalism. I mean the broader genus of white identity politics, including the national populist trend that has established stable governments in Hungary and Poland and recently elected new leaders in Italy and Sweden.

Public opinion polls show that ideas that were marginal when I got involved in White Nationalism are going mainstream.

For instance, when I was editing The Occidental Quarterly, I wanted to do a special issue on secession. At the time, many people in our own circles were dismissive. Now:

- ❖ The University of Virginia Center for Politics reported that 52% of Trump voters favor secession.
- ❖ YouGov has reported that 2/3rds of Southern Republicans and 1/2 of Southern independents feel the same way.
- ❖ The Texas Republican Party has endorsed a "Texit" referendum.
- ❖ The idea of a "national divorce," which is a White Nationalist talking point, is now a mainstream Republican meme.

In 2011, the "white genocide" meme began being circulated by Bob Whitaker's followers, who formed the first internet "troll army." Also in 2011, Renaud Camus coined the term "the Great Replacement." Both terms mean the same thing: the deliberate, engineered replacement of white populations with non-whites in our own homelands. White genocide and the Great Replacement have gone from the margins to the mainstream in the last few years:

- ❖ Tucker Carlson openly endorsed the Great Replacement thesis by name in April of 2021.
- ❖ Recent polls now report that up to 70% of Republicans believe in the Great Replacement.

No single person can take credit for all of this, but it would not have happened without our movement. So a little bit of self-congratulation is definitely in order.

Fourth, our movement is not just growing in size and influence, it is also growing in quality. For instance, the more intellectual currents of our movement which I have tried to foster are genuinely vibrant and engaging, whereas the Left only attracts boring shills. Moreover, we are gaining the allegiance of not just smart people but also courageous ones, whereas the Left is increasingly weighted with dullards, hysterics, and fools.

Fifth, our movement is getting younger. We are also seeing more women and more families with children in our circles. When I first got involved with White Nationalism, it was like going to church or the symphony. Our meetings were seas of gray heads. Now I see more young people than old, which means that we can actually *see* that our movement has a future. Which means our race has a future. Of course, youth is associated more with energy than wisdom, and during the growth period of the Alt Right, many mistakes were made because the young, energetic, and foolish were making decisions. We need to do better work mentoring young activists and creating a new leadership cadre.

Sixth, our movement is now in an ideal situation *vis-à-vis* the establishment. Because their policies are built on falsehood and folly, they can only produce disasters, which they must then lie about or cover up. By predicting and opposing the negative effects of multiculturalism and globalization, we gain credibility as the system loses it. This brings more people to our side. We are feeding and growing off the system's failures. We are profiting from their decline. At a certain point, their declining fortunes and our rising fortunes will give us opportunities to take and keep power. But when those opportunities arise, we need to have a large, well-organized, and capable movement to step in. That's what we are building today.

Counter-Currents, October 1, 2022

INDEX

Numbers in **bold** refer to a whole chapter or section devoted to a particular topic.

2018 US midterm elections, 146
2022 US midterm elections, 130, 135, 138, 139, 146
2024 US Presidential election, 142, 147–48

A
A., James, 69
Abadroa, Asier, 12–20
abortion 143, **154–58**
accelerationism, **143–44**, 145, 148
addiction, 33, 168–69, 193
affirmative action, 109, 145, 170
Afghan War(s), 81
Africa, 24, 33, 75
alliances, 1, 4, 7, 36, 39, 42, 67, 69, 74–75, 84, 91–92, 99, 128
America, see: United States
Amish, 17, 40
anarcho-capitalism, 92–93
anarchy, 41, 92; global, **91–93**
Andorra, 26
Anti-Defamation League (ADL), 122, 127, 129
antifa, 52, 127, 165, 178

Antonescu, Marshal Ion, 74
Arabs, 149
Arbery, Ahmaud, 175
Armenia, 68
Aristotle & Aristotelians, **96–97**
assimilation, 40, 49–50, 58,
Augustine (Saint), 158
Austria, 15
Azov Battalion, 49, 70, 73

B
backlash politics, 141, 147
Baltic states, 61, 71, 75
Belarus, 61–62, 74
Biden, Joe, 69, 142, 145, 146, 147
Black Lives Matter (BLM), 127, 175
Black Metal, 57
blacks, 101, **159–62**
Blake, William, 14
Boomers, 169, 174
Brazil, 26, 31
Brexit, 32
Bronze Age Pervert, 123
Brown, Michael, 175
Budapest Memorandum, 62, 65
Buffy the Vampire Slayer,

188
Bulgaria, 75
bullying, **186–87**; by Great Powers, 47; Jewish, 134; online, 184
Burnham, James, 35
Byzantium, 53, 56

C
Camus, Renaud, 199
Canada, 33, 98,
Carlson, Tucker, 34, **101–106**
Carolla, Adam, 101
Catalonia, 9
Catholic Church, 3; see also: Vatican City
Caucasus, 53, 61
censorship, 36, 101; see also: free speech
Central Asia (Stans), 61
chaos, 41, 90, 92–93, 143, 168
Chappelle, Dave, 120, 125, **128–40**
Charlottesville, see: Unite the Right
Chechens & Chechnya, 61, 69, 71, 75
Chertoff, Michael, 82
Cheney, Liz, 81; her father, Dick, 81
Chile, 26
China, 2, 4, 5, 17, 57, 71, 83
Clinton, Hillary, 136
Clintons (Bill & Hillary), 147
Chomsky, Noam, 70

civic nationalism, 74
civil society, 90
Civil War (American), 19
civilization, 2, 4, 42, 53, 57, 104, 109, 168; collapse, 168
civilization-state, 2, 26
Cleary, Collin, iii
Cold War, 106, 154
collectivism, 115–17, 120, 125, 163, 166, 169–70, 172–73, 181–82; see also: solidarity
collegiality, 41, 87, 92
Collett, Mark, iii, 60, 66, 71
Collins, Phil, 175
colonialism, 57, 150
comedy, 86, 139
comity of nations, 41
common good, 1, 88, **94–98**, 100, 114, 184–85
communism or communists, 17, 49–52, 57, 61, 68, 77
community organizing, 182–83
compassion, 79–80
confederation, **18–21**
conservatives, 33, **34–35**, 58, 63–64, 103, 105–106, 107, 108, 116–18, 119, 143, 154, 166–67
Constitution (United States), 87, 94, 172
controlled opposition, 187
Cornwall, 37
Costello, Jef, iii
Counter-Currents, iii, 22,

63, 69, 74, 125, 127, 128, 129, 140, 148, **163–67, 191–92**
courage, 166–67
Covington, Harold, 184
cowardice, 166–67
Crimea, 48, 62, 64–65, 71
Critical Race Theory (CRT), 107, **115–16**
cultural genocide, 50, 58, 62, 83; see also: white genocide
culture, 3, 5, 7–8, **13–16**, 22, 27–28, 35, 40–41, 49, 57, 102, **112–15**, 121, 142–43, **170–72**, 196
culture war, 143
cyberbullying, see bullying, online
Cyprus, 26
Czechs, 42

D

Davis, Joel, iii, 66
decider, decision, **95–96**; see also: sovereignty
Declaration of Independence, 112
deep state, 126
democracy, 2, 10, 96, 100, 102
Democratic Party, 126
de-Nazification, of Ukraine by Russia, 49–50, 58, 62, 70
deplatforming, see: censorship, free speech
DeSantis, Ron, 142

Diangelo, Robin, 160
distrust, **159–62**
diversity, 3, 11, 16, 37, 38, 39, 55, 107, 120, 141, 166,
Dole, Bob, 147
Donbas, 52, 62, 63, 65, 66, 71
Donetsk People's Republic, 48, 51, 52, 57
Dostoevsky, Fyodor, 46
drama (online), 184
Dugin, Alexander, 63, **76–80**
Dugina, Darya, **76–80**
Duke, David, 81
duty, 38, 46, 97, 185, 197

E

Eliot, T. S., 53
emotional intensity, 189
enmity, 104
equivocation, 86, 94
Estonia, 27
ethnicity, 13, 51, 53, **110–12**
ethnonationalism, iii, **1–11, 12–17**, 21, 30, 33, **37–38**, 39, 41, 43, 44, 52, 56, 57–58, **60–63**, 70, 73, 84–85, **90–92**, 128, 149–50; Russian, **53–54**, 56–57, 58, 63
eugenics, 171
Eurasianism, 28
European Union (EU), 9, **19–21**, 23, 28, 58, 62, 73
expectations, management of, 187–88; unrealistic, 196

F
Faye, Guillaume, 1
FBI (US Federal Bureau of Investigation), 138
federalism, **17–19**
Finland, 47, 61, 68, 70, 74, 75
Flanders, 27
Floyd, George, 175
France, 4, 8, 33, 36, 67
Franklin, Benjamin, 175, 177
free speech, 74, 119, 123, 125–26, 128, 130, 139
Fuentes, Nick, 123, 130, 177–78

G
Gaddius Maximus, 196
Garland, Merrick, 82, 143
Gaul, 8
Gay marriage, 33
Gay pride flag, 33
Geopolitics, 73, 77
Georgia, Republic of, 68
Gergiev, Valery, 46
global government, 91–93
globalism, globalists, & globalization, 6–7, 29, 32–33
Goad, Jim, 101
GOP, see: Republican Party
Gorbachev, Mikhail, 66
Great Replacement, 55, **101–102**, 106, 142, **199**
Greece, 20
Greeks (ancient), 39
Greenblatt, Jonathan, 127

H
Hamas, 151–52
Hamilton, Andrew, 130
Hanania, Richard (Richard Hoste), **163–67**
happiness, 112, 116, **181–82**
hegemony, political vs. intellectual, 32
Heidegger, Martin, 76
Herzl, Theodor, 151
Heyer, Heather, 178
Hitler, Adolf, 28, 55, 123
Hobbes, Thomas, 36, **90–92**
Holocaust, 56, 123, 133–34
Hood, Gregory (Kevin Deanna), iii, **2–11**, 12, 22, **30–42**
Hoste, Richard, see: Hanania, Richard
Hugo, Victor, 145
Hungary, 27, 45, 47, 73, 75, 198

I
idealism, **184–86**, 189
ideas (power of), **35–36**; see also: metapolitics
identity, ethnic, 16, 28, 40, 110; national, 3, 7, 62, 70; see also: peoplehood
identity politics, 34, 101, 103, 105–106, 107–108, 118; see also white identity politics
immigration (United States), 22–23, 57, 63–

Index

64, 69, 142, 145, 147, 151, 163–64, 168
Immigration Act of 1924 (US), 113
imperialism, **1–42**
incels (involuntary celibates), 180
India, 83
individualism, 170
Intermarium, **74–75**
international law, 36, 41, 67, 88, 92, 99
international relations, **41–42**
interracial breeding (miscegenation), 109
Iran, 63
Iraq War, 81
Ireland, 69
irredentism, 37, 61
Israel, 85, **150–52**
Italy & Italians, 4, 18, 120, 198

J
Japan, 83
Jefferson, Thomas, 112–13
Jewish question, 120, 123, 126–27, 129, 151, 164
Jews, 34–35, 45, 51, 53, 55, 58, **119–23**, **126–39**, 146, **149–53**, 166; diaspora Jewry, 49, 70, 119, 151, 153
Jones, Alex, 123, 135
Jones, E. Michael, iii, 43, 49
Julius Caesar, 8
justice, 36, 64, 95, 155

K
Kent, Joe, 142
Kessler, Jason, 177, 180
King, Martin Luther, 138
Kirk, Charlie, 33
Konner, Melvin, 164
Kurds, 71

L
Labour Party (UK), 193–95
language, 7–8, 13, 16–17, 27–28, 35, 37, 40, 131, 134, 172; Ukrainian, 44–45, 49, 62
laughter, 79–80
Lavrov, Sergey, 53
legitimacy, 25, 35, 97
Levitin, Igor, 53
liberalism, 92, 100
libertarianism, 150, 163, 166, 167, 174
liberty, 112
Libya, 67
Lichtenstein, 6
Ludovici, Anthony M., 79
Luhansk People's Republic, 48, 51, 52, 57
Lynch, David, 79

M
MacDonald, Kevin, 64, 129
Machiavelli, Niccolò, 152
Macron, Emmanuel, 69
Maidan protests, 62
Malofeev, Konstantin, 77
Martin, Trayvon, 175
Masters, Blake, 142
Maxwell, Mike, 81, 83, 90,

93–98
McConnell, Mitch, 143
metapolitics, 89; see also: ideas, power of
might vs. right, 14, **86–89**; see also: power (political)
Millennials, 169
miscegenation (interracial breeding), 109
mixed martial arts, 57
mockery, 79–80
Moldova, 26
Monaco, 6
Mongoloids, 54, 69
Mongols, 53, 54, 56
moral hazard, **175–79**
Morgan, John, iii
Mosley, Sir Oswald, 1
Moynihan, Daniel Patrick, 145
multiculturalism, 37, 38, 54, 60, 71, 114, 143, 168, 200
multipolarity, 4
Musk, Elon, 123, **125–27**
Muslims, 69, 83

N
Napoleon Bonaparte, 4, 154
Nashi, 63
"Nazis," 47–50, 56–58, 62, 70, 103
National Corps, 73
National Justice Party, 73
National Socialism, 57, 63
nationalism, 14, 25, 28, 41, 50, 56, 58, 68, **81–85**, 151; American, 16, 28; civic, 24; Spanish, 28; Ukrainian, 9; see also ethnonationalism; White Nationalism
national populism, 62, 146, 198; see also: populism & populists
NATO (North Atlantic Treaty Organization), iii, 4, 20, 23, 46–47, 58, 62, 65, **66–75**, 81, 87
naturalization, 187
Near East, 75
Neoreactionaries, 100
Netrebko, Anna, 46
nobility, 89
norms (moral), 6, 23, 36, 86–89, 95–99; (sexual), 144, 168, 169
Northumbria, 37–38
Norway, 109

O
Obama, Barack, 121, 136
Occidental Quarterly, The, 198
O'Meara, James J., iii
online drama, 184; see also: bullying (online), purges (online)
optimism, 196, **198–200**
Orbán, Victor, 34, 73
Ottoman Empire, 149–50
Öz, Mehmet Cengiz, 146

P
Paine, Thomas, 94

Palestinians, **149–53**, 164
Patriotic Alternative, 73
Persia, 39
peoplehood, 8, 40; see also: identity
Platinum Plan, 64
Poland, 46, 47, 61, 69, 70, 73, 75
political correctness, 119, 130, 140
Pollard, Jonathan 64
Pool, Tim "Fool," 123, 135
popular sovereignty, 100
populism & populists, 50, 62, 99–100, 142, 145–47, 174, 198; see also: national populism
pornography, 168
power (political), 10, 108; see also: might vs. right
Pox Populi, 152
purges (online), 186
"purity spiraling," 187
Putin, Vladimir, 2, 45, 47, 49–50, 52–53, 56–58, 61–64, 66–70, 77; supposed influence of Dugin on, 77

Q
QAnon, 72
Quinn, Cyan, iii
Quinn, Spencer, 150

R
race (biological), 13, 38, 40, 108, 156, 164
race realism, 163; see also: race (biological)
Rasputin, Grigori, 77
realism (international relations), 47
Republican Party, 105
right to life, 154
rights, 6, 14, **37–38**, 43, 53, 82, 88, **112–17**, 154–58, 177–78; vs. duties, 38
Robertson, Wilmot, 1, 3, 128
Roman Empire, 8
Romania, 74
Romansch, 37
Rufo, Chrisopher, **107–18**
rule of law, 93–95
Russia, iii, 2, 21, **43–80**, 81–83, 137; fake Russian nationalism, 56, 63, 68, 70; Russia collusion hoax, 137; Russian subversion of Ukrainian nationalism, 49, 62

S
Saracens, 39
Savin, Leonid, 63
Scotland, 9
secession, 37, 38, 198–99
Second World War, 20, 49, 61
self-help, **168–74**, 182
Serbia, 67
sex norms, roles, 168
sexual revolution, 180
Shoigu, Sergei, 53
Slaughter, Kevin, iii

Slovakia, 75
Slovenia, 27
solidarity (see also: collectivism), 170
Somalis, 40
South (American), 16, 19, 69
sovereignty, national, 5, 31, 36, 49, 73, 86–87, 98–99; popular, 86–88, 95, 96, 99–100; as moral norm, 6, 23, 36, 86–89, 95–99; as power, 6, 23, 36, 86–89; see also: decider, decision
Spain, 9
Spencer, Richard, 9
spite, 152, 176
Stalin, Joseph, 28
standards, 168
Stans (Central Asia), 61
state of nature, 90
Svoboda, 73
Sweden, 24, 109
Switzerland, 37
Syria, 71

T
Taylor, Jared, 34, 63
Tchaikovsky, Pyotor Ilyich, 46
terrorism, 156
Third World War, 20, 46
Thiriart, Jean, 1
Tibetans, 71
Tracey, Michael, 70
traditionalism, 100
transsexualism, 169, 171
treaty organizations, 92
trolling, 165–66
Trump, Donald, 33, 64, 70, 117, 121–23, 130, 142, **145–48**, 163, 199
Trump, Melania, 137
Trump Derangement Syndrome, 130
trust, **159–62**
Turkey, 20
Tuva, 69
Twitter, 70, 123, **125–27**, 163, 178

U
Uighurs, 71
Ukraine, iii, **43–85**, 98, 130, 138
Ukraine War, **43–85**
United Kingdom, 9, 20, 53
United States, 10, 19, 32, 33, 44, 46, 48, 58, 62, 69, 74, 81, 101, 112, 121, 159
Unite the Right, **177–79**
United Nations (UN), 23, 87
unity (white), 3, **39**
Universal nationalism, **82–85**

V
Vanguardism, 99–100
Van Houten, Mike, 130
Vance, J.D., 142
Vatican City, 22–23, 26; see also: Catholic Church
Vietnam, 81
Vietnam War, 81

W

Wales, 37
Walker, Herschel, 135, 142, 146
war, in general, 6, 46, 49, 54, 55, 79, 91–92, 138, 168; of all against all, 90–91; see also: Afghan War(s); Civil War (American); Cold War; Iraq War(s); Second World War; Third World War; Ukraine War; Vietnam War
war crimes, 54
Warhammer 40K, 4
Wave Guy, iii
West, Kanye "Ye," 119–24, 126, 128–34, 139–40
Whitaker, Bob, 199
white genocide, 64, 155–58, 199; see also: cultural genocide
White Nationalism, 8, 12–13, 28, 40, 60, 63, 68, 113, 154–57, 168–200
White Nationalist movement, 63, 64, 180–94
white people (generic), 8, 13, 28, 39–41, 102–105, 110, 113, 120, 126, 138, 143–44, 151, 154, 159–62, 168–74, 176–77, 179
white identity politics, 34, 101–18, 177, 198; see also: identity politics
White Identity Politics (Johnson), 100, 108
White Nationalist Manifesto, The (Johnson), 16, 108, 144
whites, 159–62; race-conscious, 175–77
wokeness, see: political correctness
Wolves of Vinland, 31
worthiness (moral, of happiness), 182

X

X, see: Twitter

Y

Yanukovich, Viktor, 62
Yeats, W. B., 189
Yiannopoulos, Milo, 123, 130
Yockey, Francis Parker, 1, 5, 6, 12, 28, 70,
YouTube, 60, 178
Yugoslavia, 75

Z

Zaikovsky, Serhiy, iii
Zelenskyy, Volodymyr, 66
Zionism & Zionists, 151–52
Zoomers, 169
Zsutty, David, iii

ABOUT THE AUTHOR

Greg Johnson, Ph.D., is Editor-in-Chief of Counter-Currents Publishing Ltd. and the Counter-Currents.com webzine.

He is the author of twenty books (all published by Counter-Currents, unless otherwise noted): *Confessions of a Reluctant Hater* (2010, 2016), *Trevor Lynch's White Nationalist Guide to the Movies* (2012), *New Right vs. Old Right* (2013), *Son of Trevor Lynch's White Nationalist Guide to the Movies* (2015), *Truth, Justice, & a Nice White Country* (2015), *In Defense of Prejudice* (2017), *You Asked for It: Selected Interviews*, vol. 1 (2017), *The White Nationalist Manifesto* (2018), *Toward a New Nationalism* (2019, 2023), *Return of the Son of Trevor Lynch's CENSORED Guide to the Movies* (2019), *From Plato to Postmodernism* (2019), *It's Okay to Be White: The Best of Greg Johnson* (Ministry of Truth, 2020), *Graduate School with Heidegger* (2020), *Here's the Thing: Selected Interviews*, vol. 2 (2020), *Trevor Lynch: Part Four of the Trilogy* (2020), *White Identity Politics* (2020), *The Year America Died* (2021), *Trevor Lynch's Classics of Right-Wing Cinema* (2022), *The Trial of Socrates* (2023), and the present volume.

He is editor of *North American New Right*, vol. 1 (2012); *North American New Right*, vol. 2 (2017); Julius Evola, *East & West: Comparative Studies in Pursuit of Tradition* (with Collin Cleary, 2018); Francis Parker Yockey, *The Enemy of Europe* (Centennial Edition Publishing, 2022), Alain de Benoist, *Ernst Jünger: Between the Gods & the Titans* (Middle Europe Books, 2022), and many other volumes.

His writings have been translated into Arabic, Czech, Danish, Dutch, Estonian, Finnish, French, German, Greek, Hungarian, Norwegian, Polish, Portuguese, Russian, Slovak, Spanish, Swedish, and Ukrainian.

www.ingramcontent.com/pod-product-compliance
Lightning Source LLC
Chambersburg PA
CBHW030109170426
43198CB00009B/546